ID0437069

From Place to Place

Also by the author

From Time to Time

HANNAH TILLICH

From Place to Place

TRAVELS WITH PAUL TILLICH

TRAVELS WITHOUT PAUL TILLICH

STEIN AND DAY/*Publishers*/New York

First published in 1976
Copyright © 1976 by Hannah Tillich
All rights reserved
Designed by Ed Kaplin
Printed in the United States of America
Stein and Day/*Publishers*/Scarborough House,
Briarcliff Manor, N.Y. 10510

Library of Congress Cataloging in Publication Data

Tillich, Hannah.
    From place to place.

    1. Tillich, Paul, 1886–1965.   2. Tillich,
Hannah.   I. Title.
BX4827.T53T52   910′.4   75-34490
ISBN 0-8128-1902-0

To my daughter, Mutie, and my grandson, Ted

ACKNOWLEDGMENTS

Grateful thanks go to Ted Farris, who edited most of the book, and to Grace Smith, who edited the sections on India and Japan. Their task was a difficult one because they had to deal with my still-Germanic English and they had to pull together passages from my diaries and notes written over the past decade.

Contents

List of Illustrations

From Place
to Place

I am not so sure that
I was not without Paul Tillich
while I was with Paul Tillich
mostly

and that I was with Paul Tillich
while I was without Him
for the last eight years
currently

But now I shed my skin
after eight years without
I am alone and my Self
without question

A Play with the Heavens

In my somewhat somnambulistic wanderings through the rituals of many of the world's religions, I have experienced the sights, sounds, and smells of liturgical exercises, but have done so not so much because I was seeking faith but a way out of any faith and into what I would call freedom.

I rolled up the road, racing the white line, skidding past the signposts of organized religion. Driving across the Egyptian desert, stopping at the Sea of Galilee, climbing the high plateaus of Tibet, descending into the Indian plain with an inarticulate desire for freedom of or freedom to . . .

Would it come to me through the image of the crucified Christ or through the gentle abandonment of the Buddha?

Would it satisfy me to preserve each physical particle after my body's death, maintaining that Life is Substance?

Or, was Zen the answer? A return to the simplest routines of living after having explored the "impossible"? Absurdity become a discipline.

Could Shiva help? The God with a thousand arms, stomping the universe, destroying space and time.

Absurdity lurked in every discipline.

Repetition was the enemy of liberation.

I got a glimpse of the freedom I was longing for in the knowledge that both terror and enchantment are entirely self-created. If I dared to call upon my powers to break through the stone walls of my self-made prison, if I dared to call for the annihilation of my so-called virtues and vices, down through the last muscle of my physical being, I might acquire a certain nonchalance in matters human. I might find a place where I could coexist with both myself and others. Self-awareness was not the goal, for there would be less awareness of the self and more self-forgetfulness the nearer one approached this pinpoint of freedom.

·

A bishop, having heard about two old men living by themselves on an island, hurried to bring them the blessings of the Lord. Shocked at their ignorance of church doctrine, he hastened to teach them the *Lord's Prayer* before departing.

On the way back, the bishop sat on the deck of his ship beneath a canopy erected to protect him from the sun's harsh rays. Suddenly, just as his ship began to pull away from the old men's island, the navigator fearfully drew the bishop's attention to something moving toward them across the surface of the ocean. Squinting his eyes against the glare, the bishop could just make out the two old men walking arm in arm across the water as though it were an ordinary country road. They had forgotten the prayer and wished in all humility he would teach it to them once more. But the bishop no longer felt competent to teach them anything. He asked their blessing and beseeched them to never worry again about learning such things. The two old men departed as they had come, their virtue unknown to them.

Grandfather and
Grandmother in East
Hampton, 1961

Grandson and
Grandfather in the early
1960s

Grandson, 1972, in the South of France

In the garden of Hellbrunn Castle

The Barrier of Time Has Broken Down
(from an airplane)

I

Stomping the barrier of time
like a broken split rail fence
space was flying before me

Treading air like treading water
swimming in pure space
looking backward and forward

Streets not narrowed by distance
trees not dwarfed by perspective
the pillars of night and day have been abandoned

Space moved in, grandiose and unmolested.

II

Faraway places became nearaway places,
the body of our beloved mother, the Earth,
exposed to sight. Airplanes hover over her,
undersea boats explore her waterways.
Searchlights in canyons for the cleft of her genitals,
psychologists measure the depth of her emotion.

One comfort remains. Neither in humans
nor in our mother, the Earth,
will there be a conclusion.
Fire in her bowels, curves in her space.
Whatever became knowledge is only skirting
the garden fences of primeval forests.

III

No past to lean on.
No future to go to.
Thy only mark the
white line of the highway,
perishable insecurity
between two directions.

IV

Tourist, the enchanted fool
tingling his madcap
with silver dollars
makes flowers grow in the desert
silken lawns by salty seas
palms rustling before his cottage
smooth roads to reach mountain peaks
and a swimming pool on the rim of the canyon
even if you have to bring the water in by truck.

Dressed in gaudy clothes to prove to
the Missus and himself
that he is on vacation.
He sends out his dollars like butterflies
in search of honeyed flowers
pleading for the impractical
dedicated to the nonsensical
while a good deed passes by undone.

[25]

At last he sinks in sweet inertia
letting a handful of dust
(taking the place of adventure and the universe)
trickle between his fingers, again and again,
like an hourglass ticking sand through
the narrow channel between two triangles
and turning it around, again and again,
shifting from funnel to funnel
the slowly sinking grain
uncounting time while counting.

The Cathedral

The publication of the mother's book threatened to destroy the trip for all three travelers: herself, her daughter, and grandson. One of the early reviewers in the trade press had expressed the opinion that the book would enjoy little more than a brief *succès du scandale.* The old woman, in lighter moments, repeated a caption from a cartoon published in *The New Yorker:* "Too obscene for Georgia and not obscene enough for New York."

The "obscenities" arose in connection with the woman's reminiscences of her husband, a renowned theologian, and according to her were only a description of their life style. In any event, the portrait of her late husband had aroused a good deal of unprofessional criticism in certain quarters. Her adult son, a psychotherapist, had called it demystification: an attempt on his mother's part to work through her grief and to escape the engulfing shadow of her husband's reputation. But her married daughter was alarmed and angered at what she considered a public laundering of her parents' dirty linen.

The daughter had never attended church unless the great man was preaching. Then the whole family would sit at his feet and later perhaps sip a sherry at the after-service cocktail party with a select group of devoted friends, praising and criticizing the sermon. Church activities were then suspended until the next sermon.

The daughter, now an adult and with a grown son of her own, nonetheless felt a whole imaginary church come crashing down upon her when she became aware of the anger aroused in some clerical circles by her mother's revelations. The younger clerics, however, seemed almost relieved by the demystification. It helped them bear the burden of their own imperfections. They could now reduce a complex terminology to the ancient Spirit-Flesh conflict which had, after all, given birth to the Master's theology.

If asked, "But why ever did you do it?" the old woman wanted to answer with a quote from Ibsen: "To write is to judge oneself"; or better yet from Carl Sandburg: "Maybe I should not have told that to the young boys, but it came to my mind and I told it just like it happened." But she didn't.

It was different with the old woman's grandson. He of the harmonious physical proportions and exquisite Donatello face (the boy violently objected to such descriptions, at the same time gazing into a mirror with vague adoration) thought of his grandfather in only two ways. First, he was the old man who never let him win at chess. Second, he was the theologian whose teaching he later learned about in school.

The boy's grandmother used to wander about in the old man's church, the one with the high Gothic spire, the Romanesque crypt, and the temple of capricious Venus tucked away in a corner of the left side of the nave. She liked to gaze at the central cupola beneath which lay the altar and the noble crystal of the bowl of nothingness that had been her little gift to his church. The ceiling was decorated with a wild admixture of imagery, some of it obviously not Protestant: God the Father, big-eyed and bearded, stared down at her while the Son of Man, half crucified and half walking on water, stretched out a healing finger. In the background a Madonna and Child and a very ordinary Tibetan Yam and Yum were overshadowed by a gigantic white dove. She would walk down the steps to the crypt to find two mummies resting immobile till Judgment Day, though the grain, buried with them as food to survive eternity, might sprout long before. But she most enjoyed sitting opposite the stained-glass windows whose forms seemed to echo the structures her husband had created in his many years of teaching and writing. There was the glory and the playfulness of his spiritual world revealed in the mosaics of fierce red and sun-yellow, in the soft blues, the juicy greens, the specks of white, and all enclosed by a black line which held the pieces in place. The

[28]

sun and clouds would alternately illuminate or darken the interior, shooting out golden balls of light or violent zigzags of lightning from the blackness. It no longer frightened her unduly when, out of some dark corner between arcs and pillars, a bleating bat fluttered or a woman appeared displaying her most intimate parts. She could even remain calm when her deceased husband's beautiful leonine body bounded noiselessly after. It seemed only natural in a Gothic cathedral to act and reenact the Temptation of St. Anthony, again and again, until, according to Yoga doctrine, the lion would tire of the game. Moreover, since in this church St. Anthony was not being tempted but was leading the chase, there was hope that he might shortly find a new path open before him.

The old woman's daughter had refused to become interested in the cathedral and seemed to dislike its presence. But it was a different story altogether, in her eyes, once it began to crumble. And to make matters worse, it was her own mother who was undermining her integrity.

The very foundations of the cathedral were shaken by tremors and, out of the crypt where the mummies had lain resting, climbed mischievous monks in loose fluttering hoods—professors of theology using their revered academic robes to lasso the doubtfully dressed young ladies. The church door, decorated with fish and doves, was torn asunder, the fish swimming busily away through the ether, doves diving after . . .

Although the daughter complained bitterly about how much she had been looking forward to the trip, she declined to go with her aging mother. She did not want to face the European relatives for fear of their reaction to the book.

At the time, neither mother nor daughter realized how right the daughter's fears were. The relatives would ostracize both the old woman and the book. "It's shameful to talk of the Great Man that way," they would say. But then they would whisper that everyone knew, of course, but why talk about such things?

"All right," the old woman said. "It's not so much fun spending three weeks sympathizing with one's relatives. So we won't visit them, not even the friendly ones."

The European relatives' life style had always been so different

[29]

from the old woman's. They had chosen to endure the trials of Nazism by acquiescing, while the old man and his wife had fought back at the price of expulsion from Germany. She remembered how her daughter, then a mere seven years of age, white-blond, gray-eyed, and brown-skinned, had insisted on playing "Die Fahne Hoch, Die Reihen Fest Geschlossen" ("Raise the Flag, Close the Ranks"), because her friends sang it. The mother bought her the record and bought herself the "Internationale" and played them side by side.

One day, however, the mother exploded at her husband, screaming that she would never let the Nazis have her golden-haired baby. She would leave, she would go as far away as possible, before the Nazis poisoned the whole continent. She was not even afraid to go to America, because her own mother, born in New York, had given her a little American flag, which she had jealously guarded as a childhood secret treasure.

When the national church had changed its colors, the husband had taken his family to America. All that he had tried to build had collapsed before the mindless brutality of the National Socialists. But he recommenced in a new langauge, in the new country to which he gave his loyalty and his spiritual power. Gradually the cathedral had grown until, finally, it stood completed with its lofty spires and monumental columns, its crypt and its little temple of Venus hidden away in the left side of the nave.

"All right," said the old woman, remembering the hours she had spent writing the relatives to proudly announce the arrival of herself and her daughter. Now she wrote them brief postcards, regretting without explanation that she could not visit after all. But her daughter remained indecisive about the trip, and the old woman offered it to her grandson. "I'll invite you to Europe for three weeks," she said, "including the airfare, and you can leave me any goddamned time you please, but from then on you are on your own." The grandson accepted immediately.

The young man lived in the shadow-laced corners of the cathedral. His childhood was as murky and as light as that of any post-war American youth. He lived in a middle-class New York

[30]

City neighborhood that was, technically speaking, also a ghetto. He seemed always precariously balanced on the borderline between respectability and decadence, yet never very comfortable with either. The old woman affectionately remembered him standing impudently beside his black friend, at age six or seven, pointing to his grandmother and saying, "She likes me." And one day as they had come out of the theater on Forty-fifth Street, he had embraced her and said, "You look good enough to be mugged," after she had refused to be escorted back to her hotel.

The boy was only twelve when his famous grandfather died. After the memorial service, he had brought his grandmother on his arm to the waiting limousine, protecting her from the crowd. One year later they traveled together in Europe through many of the same places she had been with her husband. The boy's presence had taught her to see things from the angle of a boy who was most excited when chasing lizards at Pompeii, or running wildly back and forth between the sand-brown assemblies of Greek columns at Paestum. He disliked churches, but could enjoy guided tours as long as he could stay close to the guide. In Munich, the grandmother had had to chase him down the street when one day he decided to run back to the hotel and promptly set off in the wrong direction. What if he had got lost? But it was the boy who had forced her to make a record of her traveler's check numbers, just two days before her document case was stolen from their elegant Munich hotel room.

In the cathedral, the old woman's daughter stared at the shattered stained-glass windows, dreaming of freedom, imagining herself a soaring bird flying out between the broken shards, away from the gold, the glory, and the deep shadows of her prison. But she could not make up her mind.

The last moment had arrived. The daughter telephoned from the school where she taught English literature and breathlessly announced the verdict: "I talked to a friend and she says that even if I do come along, it doesn't necessarily mean I support the book. . . . Only we must agree not to discuss it. You would have to promise . . ."

The tension between them was beginning to relax, but the

mother answered rather unpleasantly: "For heaven's sake, do you think I enjoy arguing about the goddamned thing? So, are you coming or not?"

The voice over the telephone answered with a clear and golden "Yes."

"Okay then, I will have to get you another plane ticket as we cannot dump your son at such a late hour." She hung up before a new argument could fall out of her daughter's whimsical skies.

The daughter had fluttered often and in vain against the hard red and yellow panes of the cathedral windows, but now, beneath the unpainted ceiling and dirty gray glass of the terminal building, she felt free and alive. To her mother, it seemed that she had taken one joyful leap through a golden hoop from New York to Frankfurt. She walked joyfully to the bench where the old woman and the boy awaited her, carrying a thick copy of *The Magic Mountain* (the boy was carrying *Gravity's Rainbow*). The vacation rush had prevented the three from arriving on the same flight but the temporary separation failed to dampen the mood of the occasion. She was crisp and alive despite the exhausting flight and had managed to find her son and her mother without difficulty. She had left her raincoat on the plane but seemed only too glad to be rid of it. From then on she used her mother's coat and her rainhat too, having left her own very elegant one at home.

Salzburg

The fashionable hotel was a pleasant surprise. On his last few trips to Europe the boy had traveled with the well-known American rucksack, a misshapen, overlong contraption carried on one's back. He had slept on trains or in youth hostels, wandering aimlessly through the streets of great cities, unfamiliar with their histories and unwilling to discover them. With his long hair and doubtful dress he would have been unable to gain admittance to the "respectable" hotels even had he had the money. Now he had both the style and self-confidence to go anywhere. Just before dinner, however, his grandmother found him hanging over the antique banister on the elegantly furnished first floor, wailing that he lacked the proper clothes for the hotel despite the fact that he had arrogantly refused the old woman's pre-departure offer of a more conservative wardrobe. His mother decided to scout the lobby to determine if, as it seemed, white tie and tails were mandatory for dinner. She found beautifully dressed ladies in evening clothes chatting easily with charming men in tuxedos. They were not stiff like the Germans but relaxed and sure of themselves. In the easy grace of their well-cut clothes they reflected a glamorous past and the courtesy of imperial courts. Meanwhile the son had discovered the gathering in the lobby was the formal wedding of some local aristocrat. He had even managed to dress rather decently for dinner in a good shirt, subdued tie, and wine-red jacket. The grandmother regarded the beautifully costumed guests with pleasure, recalling other weddings just as festive but with perhaps a bit more of the ancient connubial rites. In Cairo the sumptuously dressed bride had been encircled by dancers whose lubricious postures had excited the audience. In Japan the photographer had carefully straightened every fold of the bride's precious kimono before taking her wedding picture. In India the bridegroom had been surrounded by flowery, swaying beauties in front of the temple. And, in Germany, there had been her own second marriage in a black taffeta afternoon dress. . . .

Luxury had taken hold of the dignified trio of mother, daughter, and grandson and they spent hours feasting in the hotel dining room. Unfortunately, they would miss the Mozart Festival because of hasty planning, but there was still much to see. From daughter's balcony one could watch the Salzach flow, or one might walk through the tree-bordered promenade where automobiles were forbidden. Across the swiftly flowing water, the lights of a restaurant winked on the hill. To the left, on the Mönchsberg, sat the Fuerst-Bishop's castle, a residence since 789 A.D. What would Salzburg have done without its bishops? Their works, the palaces and fortifications, were everywhere apparent from the highest hill to a few subterranean passages leading away to safely hidden exits. With turrets and towers the princes of the

Catholic Church arrogantly proclaimed their right to rule. A tiny window hung like a wasp's nest at the base of the mountain betrayed the presence of the catacombs, the shadowy caves in which the Protestants had been forced to seek refuge from their brother Christians, the Catholics. The caves were both light and dark, perhaps not unlike the Dream Cathedral which certainly contained all the elements of power and death and enchantment Salzburg and its bishops could offer. But it seemed such wonderful fun to, for once, be confronted by a glory and a darkness that was now history, over and done with.

Outside the city walls, in a large park decorated with statues lurking in the shadows of trees and grottoes, lay a playful castle whose architect had made frivolous games and irreverent displays with the holiest of holy elements. The cleverly arranged fountains dared everything with impudence, mercilessly drenching passersby at unexpected moments. Thin jets of water would suddenly attack one from the most indecent orifices of a nearby statue. In one corner of the park lay a large marble table with chairs cut in stone. One could easily imagine the resident bishop presiding there over a state dinner. When the assembled visitors had been comfortably seated, deferentially listening to his words, he would give the signal. Instantaneously, jets of water would shoot out from all sides and his fawning guests would receive unexpected enemas from some particularly well-placed fountains, while, at the head of the table, the bishop sat laughing in dry glory.

When the grandmother asked, "What did you enjoy most?" "Breakfast in bed," was her grandson's prompt reply, while the daughter had unhesitatingly responded, "The view of the river from the hotel." The white-haired porter, a delightful worldly gentleman with kind eyes, must have sized them up correctly, and even his young assistants seemed to like the two beautiful guests who made constant polite, anxious, and sometimes outlandish inquiries about the customs of the hotel. Daughter and grandson were always treated with charming consideration.

When it came to planning the day's excursions, the daughter took the lead, while her son guided the happy trio to their destination. It must be said, however, that there was one fierce argument about protocol. The boy, a seasoned traveler, reacted quickly, looking at the situation with intelligence. The grandmother had asked him to walk ahead and act the guide, but her daughter insisted upon good form. She was full of "oughts" and "ought nots," while the old woman had her own personal protocol and was less concerned about the rules of etiquette (what would the public have thought if the wife had walked boldly in front of her famous husband?). The daughter, however, insisted on the social conventions as though they were moral laws. She had a fund of free-floating irrationality that would suddenly become attached to the most unlikely objects. It was as if a grain of sand had gotten into the mechanism of a delicate timepiece; everything began to scratch and groan. Some hidden terror had surfaced. It was not merely that her surroundings had become a threat; it was more a negation of her whole being. But then, after a short time, the sandcorn would work its way through the complex mechanism and be expelled. Her whimsicality would return and she would again become a firefly, whirling confidently through the world, flying enchanted through the green-gold maze of her childhood, singing make-believe songs on the arm of her mother. Here there was no protocol, only mother and daughter fluttering about like happily circling pigeons before returning to the resting places of their rooms.

The hotel became a symbol of freedom from want and a comfortable magnanimous existence. There was a room for each person with bath and balcony. In the boy's suite there was even a refrigerator full of liquor. The hotel itself was a sprawling compound with a large roof garden, many different restaurants (formal, informal, and cafeteria style), and an outdoor café overlooking the Salzach where one could sit and enjoy the newspaper over a cup of coffee. The town itself was clean and well preserved with narrow winding streets, churches in the midst of wide open plazas, an open market, and numerous restaurants and outdoor cafés. The old woman had vague notions of delicious food in a rustic setting, an idea which disgusted her grandson, who knew better. After one awful experience, even she had to give up the idea. The so-called simple places stank evilly and none of the dishes had the flavor of the past.

[35]

The meat-, salad-, and vegetable-devouring children of America could not be tempted to try the delicate Austrian sweets and pastry. They liked sharp hors d'oeuvres, good meat, and, above all, the quaint restaurants where they could sample the wine and cheese of the region. Daughter and grandson chose the restaurants each evening. One of their discoveries was a little old house in which the dining rooms were distributed over several floors. Each was decorated differently with bawdy rhymes or gauche pictures. Occasionally they would go to an unusually "ritzy" place where polite waiters hovered discreetly. The boy and his mother looked charming, were of good humor, and oozed the joy of living from every pore.

The boy took a cable car high into the mountains and returned with luminous eyes. He and his mother took another mountain tour to Hitler's alpine retreat, the famous "Eagle's Nest."

Everything was so comfortably near—just a cat's jump from the hotel after dinner. The daughter wanted to see the Mozart house so the old woman trooped in with her. The *Zigeunerbaron*, a silly, old-fashioned story from a faraway time, was performed at the Landestheater. The marionette theater's presentation of *Don Giovanni* left the three Americans cold. It might have been more enjoyable had the puppets been simpler, peasant-crafted affairs. As it was, the very mechanical perfection of the marionettes rendered the performance unimpressive. As for the music, one could just as well hear it at home on the couch with a drink and the cat curled up on the rug.

It was daughter who discovered the garden of the fools. Some duke or prince had paid tribute to his fools by commissioning statues of them for a little green park. Why had the mighty and the beautiful so often chosen to surround themselves with these ugly and deformed cripples and hunchbacks? Perhaps simply to feel themselves the more whole. Or, did the fools' sharp minds and merciless wits help their princes to a new self-awareness?

One sunny afternoon, mother and daughter went up the Kapuzinerberg whose dazzling nightly illumination had beckoned them during their whole stay. The daughter felt persecuted by her mother's Instamatic, but back in New York, looking

[36]

meditatively at the results, she would exclaim how well they reflected the mood of the day. The pictures showed a smiling woman, the marks of suffering wiped clean from mouth and temple. There was a mysterious whimsicality in her eyes which, in unhappy moments, would become the eyes of a small frightened animal staring anxiously out from the softness of its fur, wishing only to sink into its surroundings that the enemy might mistake it for part of the landscape.

On an afternoon walk through gray-green beech woods, the two women discussed their ways of being. The mother admitted she didn't mind making mistakes, was often too quick in her decisions, and was stubborn. The daughter, walking at a furious pace, her mother dragging a little behind, insisted that she had never done anything, things had simply happened to her. She would never have finished her doctoral dissertation had her professor not taken it in hand. She felt she had taken no part in her life; it had simply occurred.

Time had run out. Daughter had to leave her beloved river, grandson could continue to have breakfast in bed. The mother, who hated trains—not very sensible in Europe where they are clean, comfortable, and swift—had ordered a taxi for the trip to Vienna.

Vienna

Daughter and grandson found Vienna a pleasant city despite their ignorance of its splendid past. Unable to feel the reality of its history, the two children of America saw Vienna as just another city in a country where German was spoken with a curious accent, and as a fascinating hotel, decorated throughout in the same shade of royal purple. The hotel's deep-purple brocade tapestries recalled the pomp and majesty of bygone days. The daughter decided that the decor was not to her taste, but that was mere conceit: she was impressed. The mother photographed her grandson on a love seat in front of the purple brocade curtain. Shoulder-length blond hair dangling from

[37]

beneath a black felt, wide-brimmed hat, eyes invisible behind mirrored glasses, his soft blue shirt became a glistening mother of pearl under the crystal chandelier. She took another with "last year's mink" resting negligently on his shoulders, and still another of the crystal chandelier—glittering flower unfolding in a thousand gay reflections. Their photographs of each other contained all they wished to remember of the trip: a certain loosening of ties to reality, a euphoria that allowed the indulgence of every whim.

The old woman was reminded of a childhood fantasy when she discovered the deodorizer that whined in her windowless bathroom whenever she switched on the light. She had often puzzled over the question of who wiped the Emperor's posterior in the bathroom. Of course, he couldn't possibly do it himself. At age four or five, she and her sister had constructed elaborate theories concerning this most momentous of questions. They finally agreed that a wet sponge must shoot out of the toilet and wipe the Emperor clean. After being tucked in for the night, she and her sister had often shared another fantasy called "The Emperor Comes." They had to lie motionless in the exact center of their faultlessly made beds, hands outside the covers, and drift away into sleep in the high expectation of approaching grace. These fantasies had some relation to reality, for the Emperor's residence was located quite near her childhood home. She and her sister would often run out to watch him pass either in a stately carriage or on horseback.

Despite much difficulty with closing times, the grandson managed to find the Breughels in the Kunsthistorisches Museum and show them to his grandmother. The daughter discovered the public park and showed her mother a lake in which stood several somewhat dejected-looking pelicans. In a shady corner, old men sat at stone tables with inlaid chess boards, silently playing. The daughter inspected the little old women sitting quietly on park benches beside the flower beds. "Must we all become like that someday?" she asked quite seriously. Her mother looked thoughtfully at her daughter. Was she not aware that her mother had long ago become one of them?

[38]

They had planned an excursion on the Danube but were discouraged by the little dark-haired gentleman behind the desk at the hotel who pointed out that it would be too lengthy an enterprise. Of course, the three went to the Sacher for the "spitz" where the boy contemplated the bedraggled youths walking in dreamy exhaustion past the restaurant window.

They visited one lovely castle in which the Emperor of Rome, Napoleon's son, had once been held in gilded captivity. Unlike Versailles, it seemed intimate and livable, but in its splendor it seemed more remote from anything in America whose rich and powerful adamantly refused all ostentation. The old woman recalled the famous hamburger and hot dog picnic once offered a visiting head of state. Instead of castle building, the American plutocrat might collect precious works of art and donate them to museums, or his wife might throw fancy-dress balls for charity. Of course, the demand for both technical perfection and beauty had transformed the conception of the luxury hotel in such places as Hawaii and the Virgin Islands into a middle-class wish-fulfill-ment. By virtue of their American Express cards, flowery-dressed, lower-echelon business people were now able to enjoy all the efficient luxury American technology could devise. In Europe, on the other hand, the citizen paid for the privilege of viewing a long-dead magnificence he had never been able to share. But history had abandoned its glorious monarchs and envy no longer stalked the halls of their decaying palaces, now reduced to mere museums, accessible to all able to pay a small entrance fee, the proceeds of which were employed to maintain the tarnished splendor.

The mother recalled the inscription over the entrance to a famous office complex, built by one of the great "princes" of America: "Wisdom and knowledge shall be the stability of thy times." This was the sort of modest sentiment an American "democratic prince" would express, dedicating his project to the masses rather than his own image.

Vienna was a beautiful autumn day, golden leaves falling, roses in bloom . . . walking to the opera in evening clothes . . . hearing *Petruschka* under crystal chandeliers. . . . The people's friendliness toward strangers may have resulted from a residual aura left by the imperial court, which had once spread gracious favors through the person of the Emperor.

Bad Gastein

To the daughter it must have seemed the valley of the damned. The old and the sick, accompanied by their decrepit spouses, would walk each morning along the promenade between the cliff and the gorge with the rumbling brook. They ranged from middle-aged to those who showed their more than seventy years. The women, flowery dresses covering their heavy stomachs and heavier shanks, would sit for hours at the afternoon meal before foamy portions of sweets, ice cream, fruit cake, or other anonymous desserts of many-layered stickiness. Eyes glistening between fatty pouches, their spoons dived deep into the mushiness to retrieve precious mouthfuls.

She was disgusted by the couples who leaned helplessly on each other's arms for guidance and support. She could not see their suffering, only the horrible unfreedom of their lives. She forgot that though the Old Ones' bond was suffering, it was all they had. The way they walked, on canes or crutches, holding their heads at a certain stiff angle, made it clear beyond question that these were honestly sick people, not self-indulgent old neurotics. They were simply unable to move freely and spontaneously.

It was unclear whether or not the Old Ones had actually come to enjoy their limitations, but they doubtless liked discussing them. The sleepless nights of pain were, however, described scientifically, not mournfully, and were related with a candor that was almost detachment.

"But why must they be so fat?" stormed the daughter, who seemed emaciated beside "the Old Heavies." Her mother suggested that European women considered childbearing their business in life. Proud of the bulk that proclaimed the fruit of their bodies, they were attempting, in old age, to recapture the feelings of self-esteem associated with pregnancy by stuffing their withered bodies with food. And what, after all, do women represent to men, children, and the world if not nourishment? What is a wife-mother but the purchaser, cook, and distributor of food?

The American woman on the other hand was not permitted to overindulge in eating. Her thin figure emphasized her refusal to be a mere shell and was symbolic of an insistence on her own individual development. The American was wasp-waisted, unmotherly, and self-possessed. She was not concerned with the enveloping womblike quality of mother love, but related to her mate and her children in the spirit of intelligent cooperation. Could one be surprised the American pin-up was so breast- and buttocks-conscious?

At all events, the old, faithful, and oh-so-boring couples creeping painfully along in the self-importance of their suffering made a distasteful sight to the grandson's young eyes also. He simply turned away. He arose late, escaping in the afternoon to the skimpy sun roof to brown himself and, at night, to the movies, rain or shine. At dinner he would occasionally report, with a gleam in his eye, that he had seen a young man or woman his own age and that they had eyed each other nostalgically. The old mother was pleasantly surprised when the daughter and grandson failed to turn against her in the sudden realization that she belonged there among "the Old Heavies."

It was in the healing, radioactive waters of the swimming pool that the boy experienced the first animosity of the trip. A woman, obviously suffering from her physical inhibitions, approached the long-haired young man repeating in a fierce, staccato German the rule that bathing caps were required in the pool. The grandson, who didn't speak the language, returned bewildered and hurt from this unpleasant encounter. But the hotel manager, seeing the rightfulness of the woman's demand, explained to the boy's grandmother the hygienic reasons for the rule. She, however, took the boy's side in half-pretended outrage (and why not be outraged, if the woman could criticize long blond wet hair on a healthy specimen of a young man?). He finally capitulated and bought a bathing cap.

[41]

Maybe because of the incident, the three staged the Napkin Revolt. After smearing the white linen napkin with the remains of a greasy chicken or dripping curry dinner, one was expected to place it back in a personalized plastic pouch and have it served unwashed with the next thirteen meals, at which point the cycle would be recommenced with a fresh one. The three had invested much of their anger and disgust with "the Old Heavies" in the dirty napkins. Daughter and grandson grumbled continuously until the old woman finally called the manager, only to be told that the rules were strict and unbreakable; he would not even accept the offer of a small bribe. The idea of a new napkin for every meal seemed to him an unheard-of extravagance, even smelling a little of decadence. But a compromise was arranged and the hotel grudgingly agreed to provide the troublemakers with fresh but flimsy paper napkins. Thus was the Napkin Revolt victoriously concluded. After this successful campaign, the boy was doubtless more willing to wear his bathing cap.

Despite the bad weather, the three hired a car for the Klamm, a magnificent waterfall cascading narrowly between the rough faces of two rocky cliffs. The mother stood alone on the wooden platform above the waters, watching the sacred substance swirling and foaming in a boiling green mass of sheer power. It was at the same time light as a drop of rain running down one's nose and heavy as the house-crushing waves on a stormy ocean.

Departure

The next morning, the daughter left alone for the Salzburg airport and her return flight to New York. The boy followed two days later, direction Ibiza and the warm Mediterranean sun. His grandmother accompanied him to the train station where she helped purchase his ticket. The inscrutable procedures of the Austrian ticket agent would otherwise have been more of a mystery than the boy's rather feeble German was competent to unravel. They awaited the train in the cold, empty station café, sitting on hard chairs before a dirty metallic table. She wished she could have remained with him longer but he looked fiercely determined to return to *his* life: the young people; the adventures that his years demanded. She could still see him at age three, trudging melancholically after his mother, not much higher than a fire plug, looking lonely and unprotected. The grandmother, walking on behind, had reached forward, offering her hand. He had looked up at her with enormous, luminous brown eyes and taken it willingly. She remembered his tearful refusal at age thirteen to enter the slums of Naples or even the side streets near their luxurious hotel where the wash hung out and the people seemed poor and miserable.

The old woman suddenly thought of her husband's eagerness to wander about these same places. He had walked and walked and invariably become impatient whenever she had shown her fear or her pity. He had felt at home in Naples, but in a certain way he was comfortable there only because he was oblivious to its suffering and its hatred. He seemed unaware that the poor had no place in his Cathedral. But to their grandson, who had lived his childhood at the edge of Harlem's squalor, Naples represented the threat of an all-too-familiar reality. It brought back his humiliations by the New York City "street kids" who had robbed and even beaten him.

The train came; they kissed and parted. It had been a very old-fashioned trip, a simple change of air, a chance to take in the sights and fragrances of foreign cities. Not wishing to be explorers, they had refrained from asking too many questions. They remained tourists rather than travelers, never relinquishing the delightful sense of their own foreignness. But, most importantly, each had kept his own private world to himself. They refused intimacy and thereby remained individuals. The book had not once been discussed, nor had they spoken of the shadows in their lives, nor even of the trials and delights that might await them upon their return. They were like three strangers meeting on a boat sailing slowly and comfortably across a lake undisturbed by bad winds or foul weather. The boat would stop here and there, the three would disembark together, see the sights and make half-hearted attempts to exchange observations. It had all been in *being there*, standing and looking, following

[43]

the prearranged path. It was a trip of not remembering and not forgetting; the short pause between inhaling and exhaling when all motion is suspended. The ship had carried them across the lake in the same quiet manner, perhaps forming a few mild ripples on the water's surface. But the lake was deep enough so that at bottom it remained undisturbed.

The grandmother went back to her balcony overlooking the valley and the "Little Green One," a beautiful fir more than four stories tall growing near the hotel. The hotel itself was built so that one could exit either on the third floor, to the promenade of the sick, or on the first, to a path leading to the wide valley below.

She was left alone in the hotel with the healing waters which had drawn her there. Every morning she would descend the three steps to a little rectangular pool, resembling a Japanese bath, where she would sit on an underwater bench and let a hose spray warm streams of soothing liquid over the spot on her head that hurt most. In the afternoon, the charmed stuff would play around her in the swimming pool, following her movements, clinging to her body outlines, its softness surrounding and shaping. And in the evening the waters would accompany her long walks. She would start at the bridge, under which flowed a stream through its ever widening bed, smoothing the sharpnesses of the rocks and pebbles with a green caressing finger. She would walk upstream on a steep path alongside the sparkling, singing cascades of waterpower rushing down from cliff height in endless strings of pearls. Only there did not seem to be a downward rush; no falling—just the same blue and green transparency dancing between strings of foamy pearls.

The old woman would continue climbing until she reached a circular basin enveloping the brook in a bowl of milky green where the liquid, combed by an assembly of iron teeth, slithered over the edge in orderly streams. Here she would rest, gazing down over the fall whose music was so penetrating, forbidding all other sounds, drawing one to it with the sweet tinkling of drops and the banging of drums storming against the cliff.

On the way back, down the more level path through the fir trees, the brook lay buried, murmuring low amid vegetation thick

[44]

with circular, luscious green leaves, fat as lotus leaves with their off-white spireas standing on high heels in still lakes . . . clumps of sorrel with sturdy, crudely torn long-handed leaves and the full tail of their blossoms . . . bluebells, lighter than mountain-loving enzian but just as mysteriously lyrical . . . and, of course, the wooly, lusty heads of white and red clover pressed everywhere between high grass and low. A red-berried mountain ash tree threw lacy shadows across the meadow. Farther on, the woods became denser—blueberries, cranberries, and blackberries pressing together in a thorny engulfing wilderness.

It was time to go home. She stopped at a house on the way back, resting for an hour or two beside the fireplace in a meticulously proportioned room with sharp, angular lines. Unlike the huge sweep of the Gothic arch which attempted to swallow as much space as the sky would permit, this room was a single cube with square windows and a rectangular fireplace. It was in proportion to the scale of human activity it was designed to encompass. The host remarked that he had become annoyed with his architect's tired fumbling and had designed the fireplace himself. The old woman bent down to measure proportions and relationships so that she might solve the riddle of the fireplace's sparse harmony of line. The host smiled as he watched her vain attempts to grasp beauty with mathematical formulations.

"Perhaps one should consider one's own proportions when planning to build a house."

She ceased her measuring. It was enough to feel that a certain purity of intention had become something both useful and aesthetically satisfying. The summer was still too warm to build a fire. The two would go and have blue trout under the trees beside the lake. It would be the closest thing possible to a home meal, though the old woman remained conscious that she belonged nowhere, with neither the rich nor the poor, neither with those who dressed for elegance nor with those who dressed only for the sake of necessity. She had somehow always just managed to come into her own, landing, after the fall, on her feet like a cat, bruised but surviving.

Egypt, 1963

PAULUS WRITES

When we arrived in Cairo, there was no indication of arrangements for lectures so we decided to become tourists. The mystery of Egypt grew for me with every new sight. I asked myself what element in human nature is responsible for the most conspicuous characteristic of Pharaonic civilization, namely the drive to overcome man's finitude. The superhuman size of the temples, statues, and pyramids corresponds to the enormous hardship to which the whole nation was subjected in order to prolong the life of one human being, the Pharaoh, whose godlike character was expressed in his claim for eternal life. But his was an immortality bound to the preservation of the body. What made perhaps the greatest impact on me was the sight of the mummies of about twenty Pharaohs, a few of their wives, and several nobles. Their unveiled faces carried strongly individual expressions. One admired them, but one also felt this was no real victory over death. The faces, in their state of arrested decay, are extremely vivid and often very powerful (as a good portrait can be), but they belong to the past and their presence is that of the past, surviving to the present but not belonging to it. If one thinks of the immense treasures placed in the tombs of the Pharaohs, one is once again reminded how much their actual life was dominated by the problem of death and the attempt to resist its inevitability.

Jordan's refusal to grant us a visa necessitated a flight over Athens, to Tel Aviv. We could thus compare the two civilizations. I had expected a considerable letdown from seeing the Greek architecture as compared with the Egyptian, but it did not occur. On the contrary, I felt a kind of homecoming when the human measures reappeared in temples and statues, and the quantitatively superhuman ceased to represent the divine.

HANNAH WRITES

Cairo, September 24

Before us in startling heat and haze stretched the Nile, reddish-brown in the morning. Opposite was the Tower of Gezirah, a round building covered with a lace-like white lattice.

Cairo, September 25

A city tour—the old city walls built by Saladin in 1179 with stones from some of the smaller pyramids at Gizeh. Behind the arched entrances, under which the poorest natives sleep, is the old city. It stank. Noise and tiny children in rags. Arabs walked with violent steps, proud-postured, full-mouthed and keen-nosed, caftans swirling about their strong, slim figures. They responded readily to our smiles. Donkeys drove past, some carrying one or two women and others a man only while "his" women followed on foot. Other donkeys pulled carts while children walked beside, school books under their arms. Our guide pointed to the children, "They must all attend school now, though there aren't yet enough schools. But see how well scrubbed they look!"

We passed the university and the garden-circled houses of the rich.

At the Hilton, lovely, doe-eyed Egyptian girls served us in the cafeteria. Eager to help and smiling little dazed smiles, they looked unsure they were really there. The girls were brought to and from the hotel in special buses.

From the bridge by the hotel, we observed homecoming workers and housewives watching a television set placed in the street for public enjoyment. There was music in the streets, but we were amazed to find it came mostly from the transistor radios carried by young Arab boys.

The Nile was lavender and rust-brown in the evening. Currents whirled into one another, falling back in violet stripes, molding black islands smooth as hot tar. We watched as dusk fell. The darkness came on quickly.

We visited a nightclub in a poorer section of town. An old man, a fortune teller, sat at the first-floor entrance. I still regret I did not have my fortune told.

On the second floor, we found a grouping of shabby chairs in a big room open to the sky (when it rained everyone moved downstairs). The audience consisted mostly of dark-skinned Egyptian working men with those deep-well eyes, set so much wider apart than a Westerner's. On stage were two hilarious comedians. They sang, shouted, and poked fun at everything in such a comical way that I had the illusion of understanding. Another skit, involving a big, good-looking peasant woman and her skinny husband, revolved around the question: "Who wears the pants in the family?"

The belly dancers were next. They began slowly, walking back and forth across the shallow stage, then began to pick up speed, building to a crescendo. Arms uplifted, hands playing, hips revolving, as the music rippled through their bodies. After a while, I got the feel of the graceful, slithering movements, flowing easily through torso and limbs. The last and most sensuous dancer had a red ribbon tied under her navel and around the small of her back, on which her name, Nana, was embroidered. The men in the audience clapped their hands to the music, while one man called her name again and again, "Nana! Nana!" I remembered a passage in a book which claimed that in former times, after such an evening, the dancer was required to have intercourse with any man in the audience who desired it. This struck me as a logical enough solution.

In the middle of Nana's dance, a voice rose to shrieks of laughter. An elderly woman was struggling in the arms of her two companions, an American couple, who were trying in vain to persuade her to leave. This gray-haired, stocky-legged woman threw up her arms belly-dancer fashion, clumsily imitating Nana's graceful motions, hopping and shrieking with glee. The male audience—there were not more than three women in the room—

[49]

enjoyed it immensely, laughing and clapping their hands. Later we saw the lady and her two companions in a Coptic church walking down to the crypt where, according to the legend, Mary and Joseph had rested during their flight to Egypt.

September 26

In the evening, we wandered into an Egyptian wedding. The ballroom was filled with well-dressed people. A dais in a corner of the room was decorated with elaborate flower arrangements. Under a baldachin, the bride and bridegroom sat on two chairs encircled by flowers and children. A belly dancer was performing near the baldachin, doing all the sensuous movements we had watched the night before. The dancer went cavorting up to the couple, who sat motionless as wax dolls. She danced before them, lingering at the side of the bridegroom, then snaking about the chair of the bride. Elegantly attired friends and relatives moved cocktail fashion around the silent couple.

Earlier in the day, we had gone to see the pyramids at Gizeh. The road out of Cairo reminded me of the highway between Mexico City and Cuernavaca. A flat, agricultural landscape, the canals of the Nile, water buffalos, palm and eucalyptus trees. Children played by the water, farmers walked toward the city carrying their produce. Before us lay the wall of the desert.

We walked up a dusty path, past camel drivers inviting us to mount. The desert was an ocher, brownish yellow, the pyramids grayish. The horizon melted into a hazy, pale-blue sky. Before the pyramids sat the Sphinx, with a broad-lipped mouth and outstretched lion's paws, eyes open toward the east.

> The mutilations which disfigure it, date from the Arab domination. . . . excavated by Caviglia at the cost of an English society. He [Caviglia] discovered a flight of steps, which ascended to the monument, and also found between the paws of the lion a carefully laid pavement at the end of which, next to the breast of the Sphinx, rose a kind of an open temple. . . .

The source goes on to say that in the temple between the

Sphinx's paws was the sculpture of a small recumbent lion wearing the royal head cloth adorned with the royal serpent. Perhaps somebody had had a little fun, taking the official image of the pharaoh and placing it, so to speak, between its own paws. And perhaps again, between the paws of the mini-Sphinx were another temple and another image. The king's image mirrored without end, the infinite king.

What could have been a more efficient building than the pyramid? What form could better withstand the whirling sandstorms, the murderous climate and desert conditions? We entered a pyramid and walked through narrow tunnels, passing the queen's chamber, crawling at times, going up a steep passage to the king's chamber and its empty sarcophagus. The guide tapped it cautiously and it emitted a clear sound. An air shaft. After all, the pharaoh had to breathe. There in the granite sarcophagus had been enclosed the many layers of golden-masked, inner coffins and the precious kernel of the mummified king with all the signs of his station. So the Tibetan monks mummified the corpses of their bodhisattvas and covered them with gold leaf. Nothing of their earthly existence must be lost. In a museum we saw one of the four canopic jars containing the viscera of a pharaoh. I read about the ceremony of the opening of the mouth, conducted with magic formulas before a statue of the deceased king to ensure him the continued use of his preserved organs. He would live, to be sure, in a more rarefied atmosphere, but one perhaps only a hairbreadth removed from that of his previous, non-mummified existence. If his body remained intact, the innumerable workmen, poisoned with cobra venom and mummified with the pharaoh to serve him in the afterlife, would be safe in their king's infinity. The key words were: preservation of matter, endless recollection of life and repetition, as in the flight of mirrors at Versailles. It was still another play with the heavens.

September 27

Before the treasures of Tutankhamen we were simply and beautifully overwhelmed by the eternal presence of the young

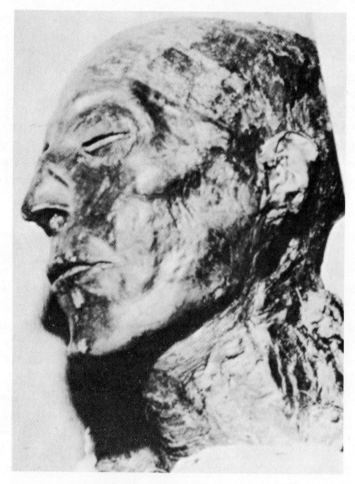

The mummy of Seti

Paulus, Hannah and their guide in the Valley of the Nobles, Egypt

god-king. On the panther, in a golden boat, in a chair with the queen standing beside him; all contained a most personal appeal shining at us through the millennia, lovable, loving, and intimately alive even unto the golden mask which had covered his face in the sarcophagus.

We found ourselves in a narrow, rectangular room, face to face with mummies of the pharaohs. It smelled musty. Or, how did it smell? Like thousands of years of surviving desecration. Paulus and I paled with the wonder of it, facing kings and queens who had overcome annihilation, who had successfully conquered putrefaction, who faced us with such personal dignity and individuality of expression, with such simplicity of being that we forgot the abyss of time, forgot they were encased and mummified while we were, supposedly, alive and walking. I had never experienced such immediacy, such nobility of presence, in any contemporary. The mummies were bandaged, but their feet and heads were clearly visible behind the glass cases. Their facial skin was drawn tight to the bone. The mouths, either with teeth or without, seemed not so different from our own fleshier lips. There was one broad-cheeked queen with a wide mouth, one diplomat with a cautious expression on his well-shaped face, but, above all, there was Ramses II, shining intelligence, kingliness, and elegance. I don't remember how long we walked there, whispering with the mummies, unaware of time's divisions.

September 28

In Luxor we wandered between powerful pylon walls into a superhuman forest of heavy columns (134 in rows of sixteen, I counted them), monumental as our redwood forests where I had had to walk far away from the trunk of each giant tree in order to see its top. The history of Egypt—that is, the history of its kings—was recorded on these columns. Richly colored frescoes, detailing accounts of the ancients' daily lives, shone from the pylon walls. And there were enormous statues of the kings. The Pharaoh's image was distributed everywhere, like "Big Brother's," to assure the people of his eternal presence.

September 30, Luxor

West of the Nile is a necropolis containing tombs of nobles and queens. We drove through the fertile plain along the Nile. In the water, standing in a meditative posture, surrounded by boys playing, were the Memnon Colossi. The guide was sad seeing them. They no longer sang at sunrise as they had in former times. They had been restored.

Restoration everywhere, as with the rows of rams and sphinxes lining the street to the temples. The road to the necropolis was a brand-new concrete highway leading between massive, reddish-gray cliffs. We passed an American's house which sat on a hill in the most deserted of deserts. It made me shudder.

We descended through a cellar-like entrance to the most important grave whose mummy still lay in its original coffin. Well-preserved wall paintings depicted every imaginable aspect of day-to-day life in vivid colors. Again the musty smell.

Paulus stumbled, his face blotched with the effort of fighting the heat and steep steps. Ahmed, our guide, helped him up and supported him to the "Coca-cola temple" where Paulus recovered over a cup of hot tea.

Afterward, we visited the above-ground tomb of a noble. Here again, in this monotonous landscape of disordered, inorganic rubble, was the ordered presence of everything that sustains man. Life activities were minutely described in the wall paintings. It was all an attempt to preserve small realities which, if lost, would cause one to lose one's own sense of being. The mummy's golden mask, covering his mortality, shone through the engulfing nothingness. There was survival here—so much so that reality seemed to have been reversed. The living became the not-yet-living, and the pharaoh's death became an awakening which seemed to express all the glory of real and infinite life.

•

We walked past houses with the star of David painted here and there on door or wall. We entered a synagogue where an old Jew showed us a very ancient Torah. Our guide was proud that this small Jewish community (about 250 persons) could exist unmolested in his city.

[55]

We saw our first mosque, walking through rubble and dirt into an open court.

One day we had tea with the wildest array of sweet and salty tidbits ever offered an afternoon foursome. The host was a dark, attractive, distinguished-looking government official; the hostess was his lovely wife, who glittered in a silver brocade, short-sleeved dress. They had been in the United States and wanted to see it again. The husband even hoped Paulus might help provide him with recommendations for American universities.

We had had another tea, in Luxor with our guide, on a sorry strip of brown grass dividing the road along the afternoon Nile. Paulus and I sat on chairs while Ahmed presided on the grass scrutinizing my alabaster doll which, according to a written testimonial, was more than two thousand years old. I didn't especially care whether or not she was genuine. She was good to the touch and I liked her.

The September heat in Luxor was astonishing. The bar, to which we retired after each effort to acquire knowledge, proved the only air-conditioned room in the hotel. We found ourselves drinking scotch and soda, gin and tonic, pure tonic, and finally, with our progressive deterioration, tea and lemon. Everyone sweated profusely, even Ahmed as he showed us the shadow of his profile on a temple wall, challenging us to compare it with the pharaohs'. He claimed to be a pure-blooded Egyptian.

Ahmed was very good to us. He surrendered his fly swatter to me soon after his arrival in dusty blue caftan, shoes, and fez. He led us to the "Coca-cola temple" whenever we needed it, he pointed things out without becoming burdensome, and he always kept a caring eye on Paulus. He was a good man and we parted in friendship.

Israel, 1963

PAULUS WRITES

Our trip to Israel was handled by the Israeli Foreign Office. And with much gratefulness, I must add that it was excellently organized. We were transported everywhere in government-provided cars with guide. Meetings were arranged, our hotel rooms reserved and paid for, and every day was filled with something important to see. Despite Jordan's refusal to grant us a visa (denied, not because of our trip to Israel, but because of our visit to Egypt!), and my two-day attack of intestinal inflammation, we managed to carry out our itinerary successfully.

For me, the most impressive of Israel's great variety of landscapes were: Lake Gennesaret, the mountains around Jerusalem, the Dead Sea, and the Negev near Elath. I was enchanted by Lake Gennesaret's beautiful surroundings, its shape, and its intense blue color. But I am acutely conscious of the fact that historical associations with Jesus, who did most of his teaching in the villages and on the hills around this lake, contributed much to the deep impression it made on me.

The mountains of Judea, on and between which Jerusalem is situated, are conspicuous neither for their height nor for their geological formations, but they are the setting in which old Jerusalem arose. Here again, historical memories colored the picture for me. One night, during a full moon, as I looked down from my balcony at the King David Hotel, over the old city walls, the roofs, towers, and clusters of trees that make up old Jerusalem, I saw, in my mind's eye, Jesus and the disciples walking to Gethsemane.

[57]

But the mountains of Judea extend far beyond Jerusalem proper. From some places one can look down over waves of hills to the Dead Sea, which is itself a tremendous experience. The realization that one is standing on the lowest point of the earth's surface produced in me an uncanny feeling intensified by the great heat, the aridity of every place that had been flooded by the salty water, the mountainous deserts on both sides of the lake, and the fantastic rock formations (like those farther north in the caves of which the Dead Sea scrolls were found). The story of Sodom and Gomorrah mirrors in legendary form this uncanny feeling about the landscape.

In Elath, a new element enters the picture. For the town lies on the Red Sea, a bay of the Indian Ocean. The feeling of having a possible exit from the narrowness of Israel to the wide spaces of Africa and Asia can be experienced by everyone who visits the harbor. From Elath one can visit the famous Copper Mines of Solomon which are located in the middle of a very rugged desert landscape. The colors of the rocks are incredibly varied, but most beautiful of all is the green of the copper-bearing malachite.

I was never on a soil so full of ancient history as Israel's. An intensive feeling of sadness gripped me in view of the tragic, ever-repeated cycle of building, conquest, and destruction. Each time, the conquest meant catastrophe for the conquered people. On the other hand, one can see in every stone of the ruins, the glorious creativity as well as the tragic destructiveness of the historical process. Such ideas came to me when we visited such places as Acre and Caesarea with their Hellenistic and older elements, their ruins from the time of the Crusades and their remnants from the Arab and Turkish invasions and reinvasions. The waves of world history have struck the land which is now Israel with astonishing frequency and violence right up to the present time.

Old Israel had its own historical development and much of it is recorded in the Old Testament with astonishing reliability. One of our guides called the Bible the best guidebook for a traveler in Israel. Of course, most important for me was the question of whether or not the experience of seeing the physical context in which Jesus lived, taught, and suffered would have decisive consequences for my thinking as a theologian. Now, a few months removed from the actual experience, I can say that what has changed for me is the pictorial imagination accompanying the biblical stories. Thus, Nazareth is no longer the small East German town in which I lived as a child and first heard the stories, but an Arab village lying on the slopes of the Galilean Mountains, visible from the plain to the south.

But, to the question "Has something theologically important happened to me as a result of my trip?" I can only answer "No." Visiting Israel has only strengthened my belief that a "de-literalization" of the legendary and mythological elements of the Gospel is necessary. Seeing the destroyed synagogue at Capernaum creates a very realistic image of the historical event but it does little to tell us how to interpret that event. From now on, when I speak of "Jesus walking with his disciples on the dusty roads of Israel," I shall know with visual intensity what that means. But the question of what to think about him has not been brought nearer to an answer by this knowledge.

The most difficult and perhaps the most important question asked a visitor to Israel is "What do you think of the country as a present-day reality?" My first answer is that Israel is a unique state. Just as the Jews as a people defy sociological categories, so the state of Israel does not fit any political ones. Certainly it is a state with political control of its territory, a central government, police, an army, a common language, law, and education. There is more centralization in Israel than in many other countries because of its unique political and economic situation. But this does not answer the question of the historical justification for its existence. One may stop here and ask: "Is such a question itself justified? Is not a state that shows the power to exist justified by this very fact?" The pragmatic answer to our question is correct as far as it goes. And it goes far enough in cases where a natural geographical basis is given. But it is not sufficient if there is no such basis as in modern Israel. A feeling for this situation underlies the idea one often hears in Israel, that the land and the people of Israel belong to each other although they have been separated for two thousand years. Some of the most passionate and touching justifications for Israel's existence have arisen from this feeling. One of our guides said, as we stood in sight of a potentially fertile field strewn with big rocks, "For too long have we left our land alone!" Too long, namely almost two thousand years! And a highly educated woman told us, "It is our land, for we have the divine promise" (given to Abraham). Here faith, mystically expressed, has taken the place of a rational justification. It seems to me that without such faith the heroism of the people in the pioneer kibbutzim and in the war of liberation could not be explained. But it is not the faith of the secular part of Israel, and it is certainly not accepted by anyone outside the nation.

So one points to the humanitarian justification for the existence of Israel as the haven for all those Jews who are or were persecuted in other countries. This argument is immediately convincing and it underlies the political decision to accept in Israel every Jew who asks for acceptance. However, this justification of the existence of Israel has no connection with the choice of the place at which the Israeli state should have been founded. Any other location might just as well have been chosen.

In view of these problems I tried to find an answer to the empirical question: "What is the unifying power in the actual life of modern-day Israel?" Every answer I received was given with hesitation, but there was a kind of agreement that the consciousness of having a common tradition, described in the Old Testament and preserved through all the following centuries, is the uniting force.

This could be interpreted as meaning that religion is the integrating force of the Israeli state and I have heard this interpretation from some of Israel's Arab critics. They accused the Israelis of building a state out of a particular religion. But this is a misinterpretation. The actively religious Jews are a minority in Israel and the more radical religious groups are an even smaller minority. The public life of the nation as well as the educational and legal systems are, however, deeply influenced by traditions that were originally religious. The Sabbath as well as the great festivals are legal holidays of a rather strict character.

[60]

Biblical Hebrew, adapted to modern life, is the language of the nation; biblical stories are the fundamental historical material in every public school; the rabbinate has jurisdiction in divorce cases, etc. But all this must be understood as a national tradition and not as an actively religious one. The religious radicals who reject the Israeli state because it does not fulfill their Messianic expectations have placed themselves in a voluntary ghetto, which they defend against any intrusion—a fact which confirms the preceding analysis.

I consider Israel a real state based on a religious national tradition which, although it came to an end in the first century A.D., was preserved as a memory and a hope. This tradition is now attempting to regain its lost presence. Israel is a national state and not a theocracy. But the national element in its tradition is inextricably intertwined with the religious element and the tension between these two is a source of both richness and danger to modern Israel.

Perhaps the Israelis' most conspicuous efforts lie in the area of land reclamation. One feels the fulfillment of Old Testament prophecies that the desert shall be transformed into fertile land. But the image is different. Today, it is not divine interference but human labor aided by modern technology which has transformed the desert. It is nonetheless miraculous in the original sense of that word: "astonishing." It lies in the line of the prophetic vision and represents a partial fulfillment of that vision. One hears often from the Arab side that only the huge sums of money given Israel by Jews around the world has made this rapid development possible. This argument, while true, misses the decisive point, namely that money was spent with extreme efficiency and was actually used for land reclamation and not for private purposes. There was strict work discipline and only the best scientific and technical methods were employed. It is quite possible that under the still largely feudal social structure present in some Arab countries, the incoming money would have had substantially less effect than it did in Israel. If there were stronger guarantees that the money would be used wisely and effectively, the Arabs might receive more outside support.

The pioneer groups who took the lead in land reclamation

projects were the kibbutzim. But so much has already been written about them that I need speak only of my own impressions of the kibbutzim and, more particularly, of one encounter we had at a kibbutz belonging to a conservative religious group. We stayed there two nights at the end of the Feast of Tabernacles and attended the Simhat Torah, the festival during which the Jews express their joy in the Law with music and dancing. They take down the Torah and dance (often in great ecstasy) around the room with it, passing it from hand to hand. This experience showed me most impressively that, for the believing Jew, the Law has not the same character it did for Paul and Luther: commanding, burdening, threatening, and punishing. For him, it is a glorious gift.

But, when we visited the agricultural establishments at the kibbutz, another side to the problem of the Law became apparent. The question arose as to how modern scientific agricultural methods can coexist with a set of laws that was formulated to be meaningful 2,500 years ago? In many cases, the only help is an interpretation (often suggested by the chief rabbi) that expresses the original intent of the Law while showing the way to a non-literal fulfillment. Here the limit of every particular law becomes manifest, as does the truth that the Law exists for man and not man for the Law.

We also spent a night in a secular kibbutz. The members have no private property; whatever they earn goes to the kibbutz and whatever they need they receive from it. This works well up to the point where the kibbutz must relate to a national life which is not socialistically organized. The kibbutz, for example, provides for the education of its members and their children. In return, it expects the children to work in areas important to the kibbutz. This makes it very difficult for children gifted in particular directions—in law or medicine or other scholarly or artistic pursuits—to get proper training in these fields. This seems to be one of the reasons why the younger generation is detaching itself from the original kibbutzim, their pioneering spirit, and their socialist organization.

As a philosopher of religion, I cannot avoid asking the

[62]

question, "What does this unique event, the state of Israel, mean in the context of the history of religion and even of world history?" Today, Israel is both a political reality and a powerful religious symbol. It represents a mixture of realized and unrealized hope. Like the medieval Church, it stands for the kingdom of God but is by no means identical with it. For the future, it is possible that its political character will set Israel moving in a direction which will end by making it an unfit symbol of hope for the believing Jews of the world. Complete secularization (with the gradual disappearance of Jewish tradition), a political transformation which would deny basic Jewish principles (such as Communism or Fascism) or a cultural inward turning which would make it impossible for western Judaism to continue its participation in Israel's growth, could all lead to such a result. Israel, to prevent such development, must remain a symbol to Jews *outside* its boundaries. This implies, first of all, that its borders remain open to all Jews who wish to come. But, beyond this, it demands that Israel keep moving within the prophetic spirit of Judaism, even though its actuality remains infinitely behind fulfillment. The state of Israel could then stay an ambiguous and fragmentary fulfillment and at the same time a unique symbol of hope beyond any temporal fulfillment.

HANNAH WRITES

October 5

Arrival at Lod airport. A gentleman from the Foreign Office whisks us through customs. Taxi to the Hotel Ramat Aviv, a non-tourist hotel filled to capacity for the celebration of the feast of Succoth or the Tabernacles. There were three hundred guest houses arranged around circular driveways and surrounded by shrubs and flowers.

After dinner, we walked to a German-style garden restaurant where an orchestra played dance music from all nations, including much subdued American jazz. A small army of young couples came in with us. They seemed as serious as if they were on guard duty—the boys in short-sleeve shirts, the girls in simple cottons—dancing self-obsessed, without personal contact. Two or three couples, however, were outstanding.

October 6

A taxi to town. The Mediterranean. People lolling about in rented, cheap deck chairs. We walked past rows of dilapidated wooden shacks along the beach (owned by people who refuse to give up their property). The water was strewn with leftover fruits and vegetables, as though the city had emptied its garbage there. Bikinis did nothing to flatter their rather heavy, middle-aged wearers. Once in a while one saw a pretty young girl but, all in all, Tel Aviv struck us as the center for middle-class European immigrants.

A visit to the house of Simon the Tanner where we discover one might study the Bible to grasp the history of Israel. At Simon the Tanner's house, St. Peter supposedly brought the widow Tabitha back to life.

As we were leaving the Casbah, we met a dog who came chasing out of a rundown house across a rubble-strewn court, three small boys pelting him furiously with rocks. It reminded me of Breughel: saints being stoned by horrible-looking urchins.

October 7

In the morning, a Foreign Office car to Jerusalem. The Highway of Courage, built at night when Jerusalem was cut off during the war of liberation. Shot-up jeeps, left as memorials, still rotted between the trees on the side of the road.

A martyrs' forest, six million trees, many of them gifts, has been planted as a memorial to the victims of Nazi Germany. In Israel, one must receive government permission and pay a stipulated sum for each tree one cuts down. The planting of trees is desired and, I believe, sometimes even required on properties. People give each other trees or, at any festive occasion, plant a tree or pay for a tree. To repopulate the barren landscape (after centuries of despoliation) is considered a sacred obligation.

Beautiful Arab villages on the hillsides. Kibbutzim surrounded by agricultural terraces. From our room in the King

[64]

David Hotel in Jerusalem, we could look over a stone wall into the Jordanian side of the city.

In the evening, Martin Buber. A grandchild brought us tea and cake in the book-filled study. Buber had grown old since we had last seen him at Brandeis. He was bent, but his conversation was alive with wisdom and insight, whether the topic was political or religious. He talked about the necessity of the "pluralism of revelation." Once, Buber pointed to a picture of the late Dag Hammarskjöld, whom he had known, and called him one of the few men "who had been able to serve the spirit in the sphere of power politics."

October 8

Paulus had an appointment with Rabbi Y. at the chief rabbinate, Hechal Shlomo. A talk about the relation of religious to secular, educational problems.

Luncheon at the Eden at the invitation of the Director General of the Ministry of Foreign Relations, our host in Israel. A most interesting, international assembly of intellectuals. Paulus and I felt very much at home and enjoyed ourselves

Martin Buber, 1957

immensely. My neighbor turned out to be an expert on Egypt. I felt that both Israel and Egypt, however much they might be opposed, have similar goals: to win freedom, education, and the benefits of technology for their people. The Arabs pride themselves on their free schools, universities, and medical care. Of course, they have made only a small beginning, having many historical handicaps to overcome. Israel, on the other hand, having had the advantage of extensive international help and no past to deal with, can progress more rapidly. But they have no free universities yet, which bothered me considerably.

My expert on Egypt told me the situation there was more difficult. Even with the completion of the new Aswan Dam there will not be enough fertile land to feed the populace. He was astonished when I told him about the Egyptian waitresses at the Cairo Hilton. He wasn't aware they could hire girls.

Paulus spoke with an Israeli on the question of what holds Israel together. The Israeli seemed to think it could not be cemented with only a scientifically oriented humanism. It needed the religious tradition. But the Arabs reproach the Israelis for their religious nationalism and I personally believe it rather unfortunate that the Israelis chose to base a modern state on Jewish religious tradition. Jewish tradition may have originated in the same space as modern-day Israel, but it is no longer the same time. Perhaps even the choice of Hebrew to bring the seventy-eight languages of Palestine together over one denominator was an unfortunate one, although I believe the language, which is not spoken by any other peoples of the world, must have given the Israelis the kind of protected, exclusive community feeling they needed after the Diaspora. They are wise enough to require the teaching of another world language in their schools. But Israeli enthusiasm must not be directed into religious nationalistic channels.

We talked about the orthodox who refuse to participate in the government and about the more liberal orthodox who successfully bargained with government for such religious restrictions as the rules about keeping the Sabbath. Tourists excluded, no busses may run on the Sabbath. Airlines lost money when they tried to stick to the rules. Cows may not be milked, nor can food be cooked. In one kibbutz, our guide explained how the rabbis got around these rules by, for example, throwing away the first drops milked on a Sabbath. But it all seemed most impractical. One wouldn't object in an otherwise unscientific state but it did not seem to fit Israel's image of itself as a thoroughly rational, scientific community.

October 9

Guide car to Caesarea. On the Mediterranean. Old harbor buildings, the Crusaders' city walls, a Roman aqueduct, excavation of a Roman town with amphitheater. We had not realized how often Israel had changed hands. A Phoenician port; a Roman colony; a center of Christianity until A.D. 451; captured by the Arabs in 640 and in 1102 by the Franks who found there the famous green crystal vase which they believed to be the Holy Grail; dismantled by the Sultan in 1291 and completely destroyed; occupied by the Bedouins in the 17th century; Moslem refugees, Bosnians, and Circassians settled there in 1884 and erected a mosque. Arabs, Christians, and so on until in 1940 a kibbutz was founded near by on the coast.

Caesarea is just a small example of the turnover of power in the land that is now Israel. The claim that Israel belongs to the Jews is unfounded by history. What moved us was the statement of our friends that the land was promised them in the Bible. What convinced us was the simple truth: "We are here now, the land belongs to us, we have transformed it, we have made it come alive again."

While driving through the country, we came to the now barren hills where ancient inhabitants had once built terraces to make the land fertile. Conquerers had razed the forests, turning good land into desert. Our guide said, "We were too long away from our land, we have neglected it for too many years." He meant during all the centuries the Jews had not been in Israel.

We drove to an artists' colony up in the hills. It was an old Arab village transformed by the government into a center for arts, crafts, painting, and sculpture. The houses were charmingly restored, painted in gay colors. We visited some of the shops but found nothing we liked.

[67]

After a short uphill ride, we disembarked to approach the kibbutz on foot as cars were not allowed there on holy days. It was the last days of the New Year celebration and the guest-houses were crowded.

At five o'clock in the afternoon, Ben D., our guide (whose hobby was planting trees), conducted a group of us to the synagogue. Paulus went in with the men. I had to remain behind in a small room separated from the synagogue by a criss-cross of wooden bars, through which we women could watch the men in the adjoining room.

At a pulpit in the center of the room stood a rabbi reading from the Torah in a singsong voice. The men bowed and walked back and forth. They began to sing, forming a line around the Torah-reading rabbi. It was strange to see these men, in their modern suits and hats, moving around the room to such a wild rhythm (from old Chasidic melodies) and with such obviously unaccustomed ferocity. The group formed a circle and some of the men began jumping up and down, placing their hands on the shoulders of the person in front. The Torah was taken down from the pulpit and handed to a man who led the group around the room clapping their hands and stamping their feet. Then another man, jumping and turning, took the Torah from the leader and pressed the holy book in his arms. They seemed in a trance, their singing so powerful I imagined them in a fiery furnace killing flames with the power of their song. And, in a shadowy vision, I saw the Jews in Germany condemned to die in the ovens of the concentration camps, knowing it, and bursting into song as powerfully as these people did now, dancing around the Torah. I believe this holy fervor, which helped the old European Jews bear their horrible ordeal, is the answer to the young Israelis (many of whom would gladly give up their lives for Israel) when they ask their elders, "Why didn't you fight back?" Those old Jews had had no homeland to defend, but only their religious fervor, which I hope will be replaced by a more rational faith in the young state's life-power.

Paulus, wearing a skull cap, had danced in the circle. I had clapped my hands to the rhythm. It was impossible not to become involved. We returned exhausted to our motel.

[68]

Ben D. took us around the agricultural part of the kibbutz. We saw cows, bulls, and the chicken coop—young animals destined to be slaughtered. It comforted little that the poor chickens seemed to feel quite well. According to Ben, they protested only when one took or changed a neighbor.

Luncheon, songs. The men went wild once more. But after the noise subsided, I vividly remember one tall man, who during the dancing had worn his hat at the craziest angles, suddenly appear, gray-suited and sober, his hat in the right place, saying elegantly and with finality: "Gentlemen." The holy day was over.

October 11

A car to Megiddo. On the way we stop at Beth She'arim (the House of Doors). An arched gateway with three entrances led to the necropolis which, in the third century A.D., had become the most important Jewish burial place in the land.

Paulus was fascinated by two sarcophagi. The first showed the relief of a man, the second that of a lion. Both combined Jewish and Hellenistic ornamental styles. We walked through arcades, catacomb streets, narrow, winding, and steep; through high vaulted burial halls containing the sarcophagi of famous rabbis; past decorated columns and a seven-pronged candelabra in high relief on the wall.

Much historical and biblical interest in Megiddo. According to St. John, the last battle, in which the forces of Good will triumph once and for all over the forces of Evil, will be fought there on "the hill of battles (so called because it has been fortified since 3000 B.C.). In 1479 B.C., Thutmose III plundered Megiddo. In 1918, General Edmund Allenby defeated the Turks there (he later became Viscount Allenby of Megiddo). A lady friend told us about the historical (magical?) coincidences which occur in certain places—Megiddo, for example, with its long history of battles (one might, of course, say they occurred because of the city's strategic location). She seemed to wish to prove the point that "events cling to places" or "places invite events."

On to Haifa where, according to a legend, Elias had the priests of Baal murdered. He had challenged them, after having prepared a bull for sacrifice, to pray to their gods to light it without human assistance. The priests of Baal did not succeed. But Elias prayed and God lit the altar. Then, on orders from Elias, the Jews slaughtered the priests of Baal.

October 13

At sunset, a visit to the non-religious Ayelet Hashahar kibbutz. The children have their own housing and dining units. Only recently has a five-o'clock tea hour been introduced to bring parents and children together. The kibbutz tries to keep its youth in its orbit. If they so choose, the children will get an extensive education after completing their military obligations. There is also a two-year period between graduation from high school and the compulsory military service, which begins at age eighteen, when the young people must work in the kibbutz. I asked our hostess what happened when a boy or girl is not interested in learning something which fits the needs of the kibbutz? The firm answer was, "We have no interest in people who leave the kibbutz. We try to persuade them to stay, but if they leave, neither the kibbutz nor the parents can help them." It seemed to me a rather serious disadvantage that parents who have given their whole lives to a kibbutz are then left unable to help their children establish an independent existence.

October 14

Tabha on the Sea of Galilee with green trees, murmuring waters, and seven springs. The main thing is to sit on the lake under eucalyptus trees, the water lapping at your feet. The Church of the Multiplication of the Loaves and Fish was new but there were ancient Byzantine mosaics showing the flora and fauna of the lake of Galilee. That fit the dream.

Capernaum. Ruins of an old synagogue on a hill amid other excavations. The guide warned us not to step into the high grass between the ruins. Later, I read a warning in a local paper that so and so many people had been bitten by snakes and scorpions.

Paulus began having pains.

We proceeded to Nazareth which is covered with horrible, modern Christian churches. A guide wanted to show Paulus a marvelous big new church under construction nearby. Paulus (usually an angel of patience) became very nasty. "We don't want to see it! We hate it!" Poor guide. But we visited another horrible little new church built over the Grotto, Joseph's working place. Descending stairs to the entrance, we read the inscription *"Hic verbum caro factum est"* ("Das Word ward Fleisch hier," "The Word became flesh here"). It means the place of the immaculate conception. Paulus and I howled with displeasure and gave a huge tip to the bewildered guide. (There had to be some compensation for the outburst of "those intellectuals.")

Paulus was sick on the way back. But we found a wonderful doctor (an uncle of one of Paulus's former students) who healed him miraculously in one day. We had two days of rest ahead of us before the trip back to Jerusalem on the 17th of October.

But first we had luncheon with an advisor to the Ministry for Religious Affairs. Paulus saw Dr. L. about the Eichmann affair and the Baeck argument. In the evening a conversation with professors at Beit Shalom University. Afterward Mrs. Sholem. We were shown the house and felt the atmosphere in which her distinguished husband lives and works. Mrs. Sholem gave us an exchange of letters between her husband and Hannah Arendt on the Eichmann case.

October 18

Call on President Shazar. He is interested in arousing sympathetic feelings toward Israel in the United States. He asked Paulus to write a travel report on Israel and wanted the names of well-known people sympathetic to his cause.

A guide took us to the roof of Notre Dame. Paulus was deeply moved. We could see the Mount of Olives, the Wailing Wall, the Citadel, the Temple area, the road to Mount Zion, the garden of Gethsemane, the Mosque, and many churches. Our companion flatly denied any possibility of internationalizing Jerusalem.

Luncheon with friends from Harvard. They drove us through the Aramaic-speaking, self-imposed orthodox ghetto. Residents have been known to stone the cars of tourists coming from the Mandelbaum Gate. Continuous notices in the newspapers about it. The police act as though they are helpless. To an eye as

[71]

unsympathetic as my own, these people seemed only weird relics from a dead past. Their beards, old-fashioned clothes, stovepipe hats, white faces, and sideburns made them appear rather like madmen. A partly funny, partly ferocious masquerade, out of place and not a bit holy. I felt the greatest pity for their children: pale and anxious, with silly little sideburns and unfitting clothes.

October 19

Beersheba in the flat brown desert. White, modern houses jut out of the rubble. The city was founded by the Turks in 1900 to keep the Bedouins under control. Constructing the town was a tremendous achievement. Tree-bordered streets (water is brought by a pipeline from Negev). It is difficult to believe it all unless one has seen it. In the middle of the desert one finds an air-conditioned hotel with swimming pool, trees, and a garden.

We continued past waterholes that had been used by Abraham and Isaac. A bewildering amount of Jewish history is assembled here.

Beersheba has an altitude of 984 feet above sea level. We went on up to 2,350 feet across the most arid landscape on earth. Only a fifth of it could ever be made arable. Wadis—the deep gorges that drain off the rainfall from the mountains—would occasionally fill to overflowing. During a heavy rainfall the water rushes through with almost unimaginable speed and power. We went up to the highest point. Reddish cliffs and hills colored from copper to tan. A plain as infertile as the rocky cliffs.

We passed the potash factories along the Dead Sea. There was a remarkable effort underway to dredge a small portion of the Dead Sea to gain access to its chemical and mineral resources. A stop at a canteen. People were swimming in the Dead Sea.

We drove a short distance, walked a few steps, and found ourselves before a gorge with towering cliffs. A path led into it, to an oasis. Palms and plants surrounded a waterhole. People were drinking the water, but we did not feel any temptation. (At that time I was rather hysterical about Paulus's health.) I placed a nice, cool bottle of Coca-cola on my stomach as relief from the heat. It worked nicely until the bottle began to warm up. Paulus did not quite approve of my cooling system.

On the way back, sunset colors made those hideous mountains still more glowingly hideous. The guide turned off the air-conditioner to save fuel. The road led down through the cliffs again.

In Beersheba, everyone was out in the streets. In the summer, the workers come down from the Dead Sea, where the heat is unbearable, to spend the night in Beersheba where it is less intolerable.

October 20

Elath by airplane in the early morning. The Red Sea was good to us; it was cool and there was a breeze. Paulus was very happy at being so near the Indian Ocean for the first time.

I bought some fish which had been "mummified" in formalin. They looked good as new that way. Unfortunately, on the flight home I lost the small package, which also contained a "mummified" starfish and a lovely, white-shell necklace. Wrapped in old newspaper, it must not have looked very "formal."

A bus to the airport. We arrived just in time for a friendly dinner back in the U.S.A.

Greece

THE MISFIT
(a play written by Hannah)

Act I. Scene I.

The theatre at Delphi. At the rear of the stage, the curved benches of the amphitheater recede into the background. In the center of the third or fourth row sits a statue (or a painting on a backdrop) of Hera, symbol of the maternal presence. There is a trap door on the left side of the stage.

ATHENA *stands at center stage. She appears cool and efficient, like Myron's statue in Frankfurt's Städel Museum.*

LEDA *sits in the first row of the amphitheater, just left of center. She is neglected-looking, approaching middle age and is a little on the heavy side. Her dress is tasteless—too much green and red—and she wears makeup, a heavy necklace, and bangles.*

ATHENA *(her back to the audience)*

Leda, you're going to have to move for a few days. The gods are celebrating Zeus's birthday here.

LEDA

Listen, Athena, I know I don't belong here with the gods in spite of my relationship with your father. But it's a little late to be telling me to move now. I've still got everything to pack, especially my picture of happier days *(pointing to a flower-decorated tablet lying on the first row of the amphitheater. It shows a relief of a swan diving down to meet a beautiful young girl).*

ATHENA

I'm sorry it's on such short notice but you know how disorganized we gods are. Just following any whim . . .

LEDA

I guess I could go to Eleusis, but I doubt I'll find comfortable rooms there with so little notice. And what about transporting all my stuff? I've acquired quite a few belongings (*pointing again to the relief*) in the fourteen years since Zeus . . .

ATHENA (*interrupting impatiently*)

I know it's been difficult. I'll send you some slaves to carry your things. You don't have to go as far as Eleusis, but you'll have to avoid the temple districts. We are celebrating everywhere.

LEDA (*grouchily*)

That's what I get for being the chief god's mistress. Nothing but trouble. And look at my daughter: a misfit with swan's feet. Some birthday present he gave her! And you, Athena, your father's behavior doesn't bother you?

ATHENA

My affection for him wouldn't diminish one iota if he were to copulate with a caterpillar. (*In a different tone*) He loves creation, Leda.

LEDA

He shouldn't forget his creations, Athena.

ATHENA

I only know he remembers the daughter who burst from his forehead, and I'm proud of it. (*In a more conciliatory tone, pointing to the relief*) I have heard Zeus guided the artist's hand that your story might be rendered in the most perfect manner.

LEDA (*confidently; she has told it many times before*)

I have never again felt anything so soft and delicate as the mantle of his feathers enfolding me. (*Points to the relief as though it were a map*) And his beak on the nape of my neck. Oh, it was divine!

ATHENA (*with a twinge of jealousy*)

So, it was worth your swan-footed offspring?

LEDA

I would so like to talk to Zeus about Ledinah. She's thirteen

[76]

now and I'll never be able to marry her off with that birthmark of hers.

ATHENA

Satyr doesn't seem to mind it.

LEDA *(becoming a little hysterical)*

Ledinah isn't one of those forest creatures. She's of noble descent.

ATHENA *(irritated)*

Well, why don't you wait until after the festivities?

LEDA *(whining)*

But I haven't been able to see Zeus for the last . . .

ATHENA *(cutting her off with a sneer)*

. . . fourteen years. Don't you know Zeus can love a mortal only once? Why not try and make yourself attractive in a new way. *(Looking her over contemptuously)* Maybe he'd go for you if you were somebody else. *(Exit* ATHENA *to the left.* LEDA *gives her a look of fury and then storms off in the opposite direction.)*

•

Scene II.

(Enter LEDINAH *followed by* SATYR, *half man, half goat. Thin-lipped and heavy-browed with dark eyes,* LEDINAH *is very conscious of her swan's feet which she tries vainly to keep hidden beneath the rag of her black skirt. They come in from the left laughing and joking.)*

LEDINAH *(Suddenly serious, she crouches down and presses her ear to the trap door.)*

They say the gods live here under the stage. Sometimes it rumbles like a volcano. Underground lives the god of fire, pushing rocks aside, breaking through.

SATYR *(not understanding)*

What are you listening for?

LEDINAH

It knocks.

SATYR

Who?

LEDINAH *(standing up)*

The god of fire, ready to burst out.

[77]

SATYR (*patiently*)

This is a theater, Ledinah, don't you understand, a theater. They're going to clean it to prepare for the festivities.

LEDINAH (*impatiently*)

I know all that. (*Animatedly*) How many birthdays has Zeus had? I bet he has forgotten he ever had one.

SATYR

I don't think he has forgotten, he just doesn't remember.

LEDINAH

Is there a difference?

SATYR (*severely*)

There certainly is.

LEDINAH (*listening*)

It knocked again.

SATYR (*hopping about*)

It's all in your mind.

LEDINAH

There is a fire burning in my head. (*Taking his hand, she presses it to her forehead.*) Feel how it is knocking in my head.

SATYR

You think your head is bursting? The earth is going to crack open?

LEDINAH (*ecstatically*)

It will spit fire and lava and we will all have convulsions!

SATYR

Who cares for the future, Ledinah? Let me see your funny webbed feet. Let me take you to my lake in the woods. After our swim I'll dry you with grass and flowers. It will be so sweet when you take off your dark rags. Forget about your parents and the knocking in your head.

LEDINAH (*suspiciously*)

You want me to do what Zeus did with my mother?

SATYR

Yes, but it will look and feel so different. (*Contemptuously*) I'm no swan!

LEDINAH (*bitterly*)

Everybody knows what it looked like with my mother.

SATYR

If it was anything like the relief, it was beautiful. But no one

[78]

will spy on us, my sweet. I'll carry you to my own private nook, hidden away between the trees. (*Enter Hephaestos, a big strong man with a dark beard, carrying tools in his hands.*)

HEPHAESTOS

Ledinah, why don't you and Satyr go swimming for a while. I have work to do here and I must descend to the underworld.

LEDINAH (*stepping away from the trap door*)

Are you descending into the fire?

HEPHAESTOS

I can master the flames. They are my tools. (*He opens the trap door and steps down a hidden ladder, disappearing from view.*)

LEDINAH (*kneeling*)

What are you doing down there?

HEPHAESTOS

Just checking to see that it's safe from fire and poisonous fumes. I must prepare the underground shelter. (ATHENA *enters from the left. She walks over to the kneeling* LEDINAH.)

ATHENA

Child, you must leave. The celebrations will soon begin.

LEDINAH (*rising and turning toward the empty benches of the amphitheater*)

But I want to stay and see my father. I'll tell him that the flames are raging everywhere. Down there, up here, and in my head too. (*Grasping her head in her hands*) Oh, my poor head!

ATHENA (*leading her to the right*)

A cool mind can extinguish the flames. (*Enter* LEDA *from the left, carrying her clothes. She is obviously in the process of packing.* SATYR *goes over to help her.*)

LEDA (*muttering bitterly to herself*)

Athena was never born of woman, never steeped in the darkness of a woman's womb.

ATHENA (stopping)

Zeus's head was a volcano too.

LEDINAH

I'm tired of being a freak. Will your celebrated father be here, Athena?

ATHENA

He's your father as well, Ledinah.

[79]

LEDINAH (*bitterly*)

The daughter of a woman and a swan; I should have been hatched from an egg.

SATYR (*looking up from* LEDA's *clothes*)

What's the big deal? You're all human except for your feet. I'm half goat.

LEDINAH

Yes, but your human part can hop along when your goat part wants to jump. But I can't always follow my poor feet, which want to be in the water all the time. No, Athena, I will wait here for Zeus.

ATHENA (*urgently*)

But he won't remember either you or your mother. Zeus has no memory.

SATYR (*happily*)

What did I tell you!

LEDINAH

You mean to say he has forgotten the delight he gave my mother? (LEDA *perks up at this.*)

SATYR

Do you know how often I put my seed into creatures? But when I awaken from my dreams and no one is there to share them with, I am empty and sad.

LEDINAH

Go away, seed sower! (*To* ATHENA) I'll remind Zeus; I'll give him the underworld for a birthday present. (*Blackout*)

•

Act II. Scene I.

As the curtain rises one sees, on the far right hand side of the second or third row of the amphitheater, a bloody Christ on the Cross. The scene should resemble Spanish Baroque paintings of the crucifixion. SLAVES, BEGGARS *and the emaciated figures of* SAINTS *filter slowly onto the stage from behind the Cross. On the left side of the stage, near the open trap door,* ZEUS *and the* GODS *stand like white marble statues. The actors could wear masks modeled after famous sculptural renderings of the* GODS. DI-ONYSUS, *for example, after the famous Greek bronze found at*

[80]

Pompeii; VENUS *in the style of Milo;* DIANA *in archaic style.* ZEUS *faces the audience and is flanked on his left by* DIONYSUS *and* VENUS *and on his right by* APOLLO *and* ATHENA. *They are unaware of the activity on the other side of the stage. At center stage, between the* GODS *and the* CHRISTIANS, *stands a group consisting of* TIRESIAS, *wearing a brown toga, a* PHILOSOPHER, *in a gray one,* EROS, *and his twin brother,* THANATOS, *who carries an extinguished torch held upside down. As the scene opens,* LEDINAH *rushes from her place by the first row of the amphitheater (just left of center), where she has been kneeling beside her packing mother, and falls at* ZEUS's *feet, embracing his knees.*

LEDINAH

Father and God, help me. I am your child.

ZEUS *(unresponsive)*

God of Light, my sight is failing, describe me what you see.

APOLLO

I see a lonely child with swan's feet kneeling before you and refusing to move.

LEDA *(arising and drawing near)*

Remember me?

ZEUS

Enlighten me, Athena.

ATHENA

It's an old mistress. Her daughter is at your feet.

VENUS

The mother is a rather unattractive, neglected-looking mortal.

LEDA *(standing before him)*

Zeus, you may not know my daughter but you must remember me. Fourteen years ago you dived into my beauty as a divinely soft-feathered swan.

VENUS

The old woman, forgotten for fourteen years. An ugly duckling for a daughter. How could you, Zeus? Where were you all that time?

ZEUS

Imagining, inventing, creating. Pictures floated through my mind and materialized at a whim. Ah, the dreams of a god;

[81]

becoming fruit and crystal, man and beast. The ecstasy of fulfillment, of realizing every thought form into fleshy splendor. Creating Athena's coolness, my coolness in her; Venus's softness, my softness in her; and in Diana my love of the hunt. Becoming myself in the soft body of a swan, in the brutal power of a bull. Giving life, that is where I was.

LEDINAH

Take away my swan's feet, Father.

LEDA (*with a despairing gesture*)

Please, Zeus, heal my daughter.

ZEUS

I can't change creation at your pleasure.

LEDINAH (*beside herself*)

A miracle, my lord, please, a miracle!

ZEUS

I cannot change your fate. Though I was the cause of your beginning, you must endure your end.

LEDA and LEDINAH (*together*)

Have pity, Zeus, please have pity! Give us a miracle!

ZEUS (*arrogantly*)

It is not for me to help those frowned upon by fortune. And, like it or not, I have my own fate to endure.

(ATHENA, *taking* LEDA *and* LEDINAH *firmly by the hand, leads them toward the Christian crowd, by now fully assembled.* SATYR *enters left and hovers uncertainly in the background, staring after* LEDINAH.)

ATHENA (*to* LEDA *and* LEDINAH)

Don't you understand? Zeus has been smitten by blindness. (*Letting go of* LEDA *and* LEDINAH *she returns to* APOLLO'S *side.*)

TIRESIAS (*stepping toward* LEDINAH *and her mother*)

Go to the crucified one, Ledinah. He will have pity.

LEDINAH (*still gazing imploringly at* ZEUS)

Have pity on me, Father!

TIRESIAS (*to* LEDINAH, *pointing to the* CHRISTIANS)

They will take you in.

LEDINAH (*as* LEDA *joins the crowd behind the Cross*)

What can they offer me?

TIRESIAS

Pity, which is all you crave. You will never be beautiful but He (*points to the Cross*) will teach you to be proud of being a misfit. You will receive plenty of fatherly love and remain wrapped in an eternal childhood.

LEDINAH (*triumphantly*)

Farewell, you beauties; good-bye, you tragedy-loving gods. I have found my saviour. (*She waddles to the foot of the Cross and prostrates herself before it. Spotlight on* CHRIST's *bloody face and on* LEDINAH, *whose webbed feet have been shed like an ugly skin. She has human feet. The* CHRISTIANS *move in front of the Cross and huddle around* LEDINAH *who rises to her feet. A steadily increasing rumble becomes audible from beneath the stage.*)

LEDA (*embracing her daughter*)

He has changed the laws of nature for her sake!

CHRISTIANS (*muttering*)

A miracle, it's a miracle, a healing miracle!

LEDINAH (*facing the Cross*)

You have taken my ugliness upon yourself. I am yours. (*The crowd begins to sing Christian melodies. The first is "Take My Hands and Guide Me," the second, "Haupt Voll Blut und Wunden." The singing blends with the ever louder volcanic noises coming from beneath the stage. Both will continue throughout the rest of the play and will reach a crescendo a few seconds after the final blackout.* HEPHAESTOS *appears from the waist up in the open trap door.*)

HEPHAESTOS (*to* ZEUS)

My lord, the hour has come. (*He descends again.*)

ZEUS (*still flanked by* DIONYSUS *and* VENUS *on his left and* APOLLO *and* ATHENA *on his right*)

Come, brother DIONYSUS, you must guide me to the underworld. My birthday has become our death day. Our images will be defaced under the new god's regime. Our power and our beauty will become naught but a shadowy memory or a story too rarely told. But always there will remain a few children of Zeus, the brothers and sisters of Athena, who will seem strangers to the new god. *They* will not seek shelter in an afterlife nor demand

[83]

release from Fortune's bonds. (*Guided by* ATHENA *and* DIONYSUS, ZEUS *walks slowly to the open trap door.* APOLLO *and* VENUS *follow. The lights are extinguished on the left side of the stage rendering the* GODS *invisible.* SATYR, EROS, THANATOS *and a* PHILOSOPHER *can, however, still be seen. They are standing in a group at center stage.*)

SATYR (*hopping over to the Christian side*)

There will always be woods and lovers of goat people.

THANATOS (*removes his toga, and throws it aside. He takes off his wig and mask, revealing a skeleton mask beneath. He has become a Baroque image of* DEATH.)

Socrates chose the hour of his departure. He welcomed Death as a noble fulfillment of his fate. But I bring the unexpected violent end, striking at random in the crowd.

EROS (*to* PHILOSOPHER)

My friend, you must blind me. I cannot bring myself to bring desire to undesirables.

PHILOSOPHER

EROS, I will bind shut your eyes. From now on you will shoot your arrows indiscriminately into the crowd. As for me, this religion represents a new beginning in which I shall take no part.

(*Blackout for about ten seconds. As the stage lights come back up the* CHRISTIANS *have spread over the entire stage as they continue grotesquely singing* "Haupt Voll Blut und Wunden." *The* GODS *and* PHILOSOPHER *have disappeared.* DEATH *stands grimly over the scene in the second row of the amphitheater.* EROS, *wearing a sleeping mask, has turned his back on the proceedings.* LEDA *and* LEDINAH *are among the most enthusiastic of the Christian carousers. After ten or fifteen seconds of this there is a final blackout and the curtain falls.*)

THE END

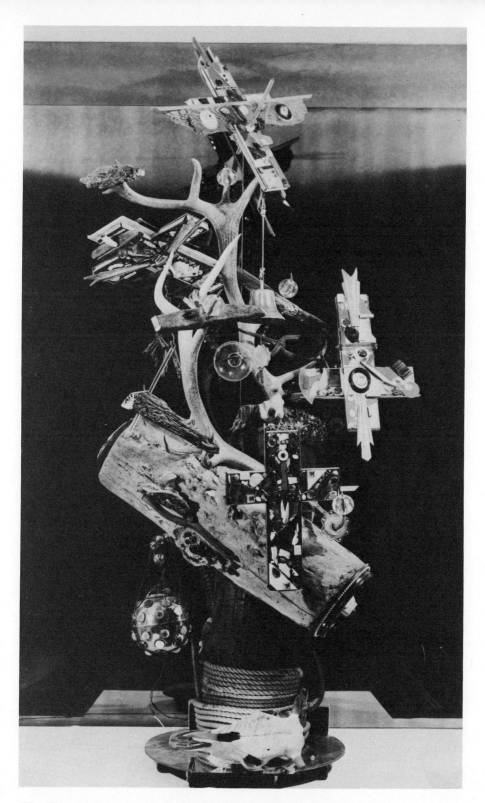

The Tree of Crosses, a sculpture by Alfonso Ossorio (*Geoffrey Clements*)

SOCRATES
(a speech delivered by Paulus)

If we want to know what Socrates means, we look at Plato. This
shows that there are cases in which the decisive thing is the image
of a personality, through which he had his effect on all following
generations, and that it is *not* important—fundamentally important, at least—to find out exactly how this image that Plato gives
came into existence. For the interpretation of the meaning of
Socrates, the figure in the Platonic *Dialogues* is decisive—
especially the early *Dialogues*.

The sources agree on the one point—that in the case of
Socrates, not the results of his thinking are decisive, but his
being; and this is an analogy to Jesus as the Christ; it is always the
being of Jesus as the Christ to which all the little stories that we
have in the New Testament point, and not so much a collection
of doctrines. In the pre-Socratics, in Democritus, we have a
collection of teachings; in Socrates, we have being, power of
being, radiation of being. One could say that in Socrates
philosophy is incarnated in a personal existence. The *spirit*, the
meaning of philosophy, is identical with this personality. And
this is what made him so great. If you ask for the results, then you
must say: partly we don't know them, partly they seem even to
sound banal, partly they are identical with what Plato did with
them. If you look at the *existence* of his being, then he surpasses
by far any other Greek philosopher, including Plato and Aristotle, because from the point of view of *being* he is the
embodiment of the spirit of philosophy.

What is this spirit? This spirit in Socrates is the honest
objective research, and actions in which the results of this

research are actualized in practice. But this objectivity had a very special character in Socrates. In the Archaic period it was the attempt to dig into the substance of all things, without considering the subject. In the transitory period we have discussed in the last two hours, in Democritus and Sophists, we find disillusion about the possibility of digging into reality and reflections about the subjectivity. In Socrates we have a third step, a step in which the subjectivity itself now subjects itself to objective norms, to the logical and ethical norms. And that's what Socrates did. In fighting against the Sophists, whose doubt about natural philosophy he shared, he discovered a new norm, a new validity in the realm of subjectivity, in logic and ethics. Socrates subjected himself to the necessity of the form, of the cognitive form, and of the ethical form. He was not interested in the mass of scientific material which some of his predecessors had brought to light. He turned away from this. He was in every respect an enemy of the capitalism of knowledge—collecting knowledge as capital. This didn't interest him at all. He didn't deliver knowledge, but he shaped the consciousness toward asking for truth and toward subjecting oneself to practical and theoretical truth. This makes him for all periods of history the greatest philosophical educator. The great educator is he who introduces, or, better, initiates, you into the attitude of research and of subjection to the truth. Therefore one of the main forms of his working, his talking with people, was communicating *not contents* but the *experience of discovering truth.*

In this sense Socrates was the greatest of the creative educators, and a witness to this is that there were four great Socratic schools, all using his name as a point of reference—the Cynics, the Hedonists, Plato, and Aristotle. All four claimed this man for themselves, just as the teachers of the Corinthians (in Paul's letter to First Corinthians) produced four schools of theological thought, and Paul gives the same answer that Socrates probably would have given, namely that it is not the difference of the schools that is ultimately decisive, but the participation in the Christ; and Socrates would have said: in the spirit of philosophy, which is embodied in me—but he himself would never have said this.

[87]

Now in order to educate somebody in this way, you must educate him to autonomy. A radical criticism of the Sophists is taken up by Socrates, and only on this basis is his trial understandable, because in all other respects he was against the Sophists. What does autonomy mean? It is derived from *autos* and *nomos* (self-law). It means that someone who starts thinking and asking should not be dependent on religious, political, or even philosophical authorities. He should start by himself. He should make the experience of asking and discovering. But autonomy is also *nomos*—law, norm, rational necessity. And here the step from Socrates to the Sophists becomes visible. The element of will-to-power, of arbitrariness, which we found in the Sophists, is declined by him. The *autos*, the self, is subjected to the *nomos*, to the law, which he finds in his own reason, in the rational structure of the human mind. The law is not heteronomous, is not strange to us, it is our own law, the law of our essential being. It is nothing from outside, but' it is inner necessity and can be found and discovered.

On the other hand, he demands subjection to the inner necessity of the form, negation of the authority in principle— even the state law and the state religion are not true: they must be judged by autonomous reason; but even if this judgment is negative it is better to subject oneself to them than to try to escape their demands. He accepts tradition, but he is not traditionalistic. He doesn't confuse tradition with truth, although he accepts tradition as a necessity of life.

How do we come to this objective truth in the realm of the mind, of the subject? Through dialogue—*dialegesthai*: talking with each other about problems; from which "dialectics" is derived. We have found objective dialectics in Heraclitus and Zeno the Elead. There, reality seemed to be in tension with itself, and not only we who *talk* about reality. Now dialectics become subjective—which doesn't mean willfulness: subjects, interlocutors, take up the "yes" and "no," which in Heraclitus is in nature itself. Now the "yes" and "no" are taken up by different persons who talk about truth with each other, and in this way it is possible to find truth. In the first stage, that of Heraclitus, things deny each other. The substance, however, remains. Now opinions deny each other, but the true concept remains and can be found. If we deal with the substance of reality, with its nature, then we have objective dialectics whenever we want to describe reality adequately. If we look for the right concept, then we are in the realm of subjective dialectics, the dialectics by the dialogue, by talking with each other.

In Socrates we have the discovery of subjective dialectics, dialectics in terms of dialogue. This is the basis for the Platonic dialogues.

The way of finding a concept is a description and a definition. It is not a matter of observations of nature or of experiments, but it is the way of examples, examples in which the essence of a traditional concept is analyzed. For instance, if you want to know what courage is, you cannot find out by physical observations—you can perhaps find that some physiological movements occur in the body, but the essence of courage cannot be found in this way. In order to find it you must look at deeds which are traditionally called courageous, and then you must find the common denominator of them, that which makes courage courage, in all these cases. This of course presupposes that in the traditional language truth is implied and that it is possible to develop it out of the traditional language.

The methodological tools of the Socratic dialogue are irony and, metamorphically, what he calls "midwifery." Irony means the dissolution of opinions. Ironically, Socrates in the early Platonic dialogues drives the Sophists to the consequences of their opinions; and when they are in the ditch, they have become ridiculous. They are objects of his superior ironic method of driving them to give up their arrogant willfulness. They have to become serious by seeing that their opinions are not worth anything. This is the day of irony, which we all use sometimes in our discussions toward each other, or I toward you, or even more, you toward me—driving toward the consequences of the first opinion, showing their contradictions, their impossibilities, and perhaps even their nonsense character. This is the one way of doing it.

The other way, even more important, is what is given in the symbol of midwifery, i.e., the teacher does not give new contents but helps to develop the insights of the pupil, which perhaps neither the pupil nor the teacher knows. The doctor who helps [in the delivery of] new babies . . . does not know about it; it belongs to the wife, to the mother. In the same way, Socrates thinks the truth he produced, for example, in Plato, is not the truth that he, Socrates, has imposed on Plato, but the truth that which, under the helping creativity of the great educator, comes out of the pupil himself. And this of course is the highest form of teaching: to get something out of the pupil which even the teacher doesn't know.

In the Socratic ethics we have the idea, which has often been quoted, that virtue is teachable, that if our intellect is enlightened, then it is able to direct our will. The thing about which Socrates speaks, when he says virtue is teachable, is not a matter of calculating intellect. Knowledge, for Socrates, is a matter of the total man, implying the practical obedience to norms. Knowledge is an act of the *whole* human being, implying will and feeling. The teacher, therefore, is, as I said already, leader: he develops something. For Socrates, knowledge is knowledge of wisdom and not of *scientia*, of science. These two concepts—wisdom and science *(gnosis* and *episteme)*—must be distinguished in order to understand what Socrates means. Today we have a better way of understanding this than perhaps people did fifty years ago. We have learned from depth psychology the concept of insight. This concept goes beyond an intellectualistic knowledge. The contrast is very clear in the case of a psychoanalysis: someone who has studied everything about psychoanalysis goes to a psychoanalyst. He knows everything about it in terms of *scientia, episteme*, science, rational knowledge. And the analyst is horrified because he knows nothing will be more difficult than to help this man, because in order to be helped—in order to develop virtue, in the concept of Socrates—he must have insights. But his knowledge of psychoanalysis will prevent him from having insights. Insights are knowledge by participation in that which is unconscious in us, in that which is repressed in us, in the disorders of our whole personal development. This insight has the character of a sudden flash of lightning. It has the character of existential transformation and that is what Socrates means. So don't use this shallow contrast between Socrates and

Paul, if you intend to be fair. . . . The aim of ethical acting is the good. The good as defined by Socrates is what is good for-the-sake-of; more exactly: what is useful.

The question then is: useful for whom? Useful for what purpose? Socrates never gave the answer to this question. He did not give a system of values. This remains a problem for all his followers.

Japan, 1960

PAULUS WRITES

Our trip to Japan was the result of an invitation from the Committee for Intellectual Interchange, which has branches in both New York and Tokyo.

The night flights from Honolulu to Tokyo and back were a new experience for us. The flights were made even more interesting by the fact that, because of the International Dateline, we lost the second of May on our way over and repeated the tenth of July on our way back.

We arrived at Tokyo airport at six A.M. and it is a comment on Japanese hospitality that even at this hour most members of the committee were present to receive us. Fortunately, some of them spoke excellent English and were able to help us from the moment of our arrival to our departure. Throughout the trip, Hannah and I were reduced to the state of babies. We could neither read, nor write, nor speak without an interpreter. We could not travel alone or even eat in a Japanese house or restaurant without assistance. But there was always someone to help with friendliness and often with seemingly infinite patience.

The nine weeks were broadly divided into five and one half weeks in Tokyo, three weeks in Kyoto, and several days in Karuizawa, a mountain resort. From Tokyo and Kyoto, we visited other places of cultural or religious importance such as Kamakura, Nara, Nikko, Sendai, the Ise shrine and so forth. Our program was carefully arranged by the Interchange Committee and they did a magnificent job choosing from among innumerable possibilities those of greatest importance. They had to refuse

[93]

ᴊmany requests for lectures, discussions, and interviews and this
was often not easy. I realized in the first few days that I could not
use any of my American lectures without making drastic changes
demanded by the Japanese cultural, religious, and political
situation.

At the International House, a meeting place for Japanese and
foreign scholars, we met Americans, Europeans, Japanese, Indians, etc. Some were old and some new acquaintances. But most
important were the leaders and staff of the House itself. Professor
Takagi, Chairman of the Interchange Committee, and Mr.
Matsumoto, the Director of the International House, were the
guiding spirits of both institutions. They combine the best of the
aristocratic Japanese tradition with a deep understanding of
Western culture. Both men play an important role in the public
life of Japan although they belong to a small group of non-
denominational Christians, the so-called Non-Church Movement. Politically they are close to what we have called Religious
Socialism, a religiously founded, democratic socialism. Of course,
they are sharp critics of the ruling, conservative party.

Our awareness of racial differences quickly disappeared. The
people we met soon lost their original strangeness and appeared
to us only in their personal differentiation. It was much more
difficult to penetrate the barriers of tradition and culture. I felt
this acutely in the preparation of my lectures and during the
discussion periods.

As for the language problem, every lecture, speech, and
discussion had to be translated. I would speak for about three
minutes and then sit down to hear my thoughts expressed in
ununderstandable sounds over which I had as little control as I
did over the texts of my books which have appeared in Japanese.
For this system to work, I had to develop my ideas to the
translator for about an hour before each lecture. The lectures
themselves lasted from two to two and one half hours.

For the Japanese students this was obviously not too much.
They listened attentively to both the English and Japanese
presentations. About one in five had some knowledge of English
but even they needed the Japanese translation. I shall never
forget the scene at Kyoto University where some students

[94]

listened from outside the windows of the overcrowded lecture hall for more than two hours, holding umbrellas against the intermittent rainstorms. Unfortunately, I had little occasion to talk with the students, partly because of my tight schedule but also because of their own hesitation to ask questions in the presence of their professors.

The lectures most requested centered on the problems of "Religion and Culture" and the "Philosophy of Religion." The others were: "Philosophy and Theology," "The Influence of Philosophy on My Thought," "Principles of Religious Socialism," "The Spiritual Foundations of Democracy," and "Essentialism and Existentialism." The lectures were delivered at about ten universities, including Tokyo and Kyoto Universities. In each case, a colleague was given me as an "interpreter" (the more expressive word for translator). Professor Ariga, an active Christian and alternate delegate to the Central Committee of the World Council of Churches, often served in this capacity.

Before each lecture we would have a cup of green tea in the dean's or president's office. Afterward, there was frequently an elaborate dinner given by the president in a Japanese restaurant or club.

We were invited to many such dinners, which often ran up to fourteen courses, each of them so small that one could eat almost everything. Many kinds of fish, including raw fish, and innumerable vegetables would appear, invariably served by kneeling girls in kimono and obi. The guests sit on low pillows, legs under their bodies, a position to which one must be accustomed from early years on. Hannah, because of her regular yoga exercises, was able to sit in this fashion. I, or more exactly my legs, found changing methods of survival. The wooden sticks for grasping the food were beyond my skill so that I usually asked for a fork. The seating arrangement is exactly regulated by age and rank and it sometimes takes five minutes or more before the right person is found and persuaded to take a "better" seat (nearer the guest of honor). The host keeps in the background and directs the procedures. After dinner, the guest of honor rises and the whole thing is finished.

Many other social forms recall the feudal period. The

repeated deep bows corresponding to our handshake, the gracious politeness of subordinates, the dependence on the family, the reverent attitude of woman to man, her exclusion from her husband's social life, the ceremonial character of festivals, for example weddings—of which we saw several during our stay at the International House (but only on astrologically favored days)—the students' dependence on their teachers (despite the recent revolutionary outbreaks), and the custom of farewell gifts (given even after dinner invitations!) from which Hannah and I benefited abundantly.

But all this is under continuous attack by—and in an ultimately hopeless state of defense against—Western forms of life. With the democratization of life and the progression of the spirit of industrial society, these feudal remnants are rapidly disappearing. An extremely intelligent and well-educated young man asked me, "What can our traditions mean to us when we live a daily life which has no relation to them?" Another factor is the entrance of women into business life, a phenomenon which dates only from the last war and has helped greatly to undercut the feeling of inequality which had seemed so natural to the Japanese woman.

A third element in the crumbling of paternal traditions is the development of unionized labor and its victories in the area of large-scale enterprises. But this is only one sector of the economy. Driving through the smaller main streets of the big cities, one sees one tiny store after another in endless rows, each selling special types of goods, and one wonders how they all survive. But they do survive. One can often look through the store back into their private rooms and see them eating, playing, and working. These stores are family enterprises. They nourish the family spirit and with it the old traditions. The situation of the peasants, who make up the majority of the population, is similar. These two groups, supported by big business, have produced the conservative majority which will probably continue to rule Japan for the foreseeable future.

As I was in Tokyo during the critical three weeks of the June 1960 disturbances, I think it appropriate to give my impressions of the political situation there. These impressions are the result of many discussions with both Japanese and foreigners who were deeply involved in the events and their interpretation in the world press. I will sum up my ideas as follows. First, the June demonstrations were neither anti-Western nor anti-American. Secondly, they were organized by Communist student groups under the leadership of its radical, "Trotskyite," majority. Thirdly, the vast majority of the participants in the demonstrations were non-Communist students, often accompanied by their professors and workers who marched under the leadership of the two Socialist parties. Fourthly, the motive of these groups was a double one: fear of becoming involved in a new war by the security pact and the entire Left's hostility toward the undemocratic attitude displayed by the Kishi government, especially as regards the manner in which it pushed through the security pact. Fifthly, the anti-American acts of violence were caused by the belief that President Eisenhower, through his intended state visit, had become a tool of the party politics of Kishi.

These statements require some comment. One must first point out that there is an astonishing pro-American feeling in Japan. General MacArthur, the commander of the occupation forces, is virtually a Japanese hero. They have not forgotten who liberated them from the hated Tojo (a name that has a sound similar to Hitler's in Germany) government, nor who gave them a constitution which is democratic yet does not remove the symbolic function of the emperor. This basic feeling was not changed by the recent events, but there was resentment (felt as much by Americans as Japanese) over the uninformed, oversimplified, official American interpretation, as well as over American newspaper stories giving the impression there can be only one cause for anything negative, namely Communist propaganda. Great relief was felt by both Americans and Japanese when some senators and representatives of the State Department corrected the first misleading reports.

The attitude of the overwhelming majority of the Japanese people toward Communism is negative. But there are some unique elements in the Japanese situation as, for example, their relationship to China of fifteen hundred years' standing. China is

[97]

called "the Continent" and is the ultimate source of Japan's culture and religion. The founders and saints of the great Buddhist sects are Chinese. China is the mother country, she remained so during the Chinese-Japanese war, and she has not lost her influence despite being conquered by Communism. This emotional element should not be underestimated.

Many people seem to have participated in the demonstrations for the emotional thrill. But what surprised me was the predominance of students in the demonstrations. We were told they consider themselves the nation's future leaders with much more confidence than is the case in America. They will become the "mandarins" in the social hierarchy and they are sure of it. This is, however, a totally un-Marxist feeling dependent on the memory of the old bureaucratic hierarchies in both Japan and China.

Some Japanese observers were very glad the students had finally awakened from their political indifference. Without passionate support from at least some important groups the young Japanese democracy cannot develop. This also at least partly explains both the direct and indirect participation of a large number of professors in the demonstrations. Many of them were moderate Socialists and attempted to exercise a moderating influence. Few were actual Communists. These points are illustrated by the fact that, on the day of the most violent demonstrations, the large lecture hall at Tokyo University in which I was speaking on "Religion and Culture" was filled beyond its capacity. The students listened attentively from three-thirty to six o'clock before some of them left for the demonstrations, while Hannah and I were the dinner guests, along with several other professors, of the president of the university (who later got into trouble for making an anti-Kishi statement).

Some of our friends regretted that we came at this critical period and were afraid something might happen to us. But that was out of the question. It was true that attendance at my lectures could have suffered because of the demonstrations, but even this did not occur. In fact, both students and professors were *more* open to questions about the ultimate problems to which the world historical and national problems were pointing.

[98]

And for me, the entire experience was a first-rate introduction to the social and political situation in the Far East, and it provided a new look at the world political situation in general.

Our visits to Japan's temples and shrines had in most cases a character quite unlike that of the average tourist's. We were always accompanied by one or more colleagues and sometimes by art experts. We were invariably received at the entrance by a priest or the head of the temple or shrine and, either before or after the visit, we were invited to take a ceremonial tea with him. This tea is a very strong, bitter beverage prepared from special tea leaves in an exactly defined process. Because of their age and beauty, the teacups are often worthy of being museum pieces. The cups contain about three and a half gulps, which is sufficient to revitalize you. A second cup, as I discovered, is not good for the heart. The tea is preceded by a sweet, which was much too sweet for our taste and which is supposed to mix in the mouth with the bitterness of the tea. All this occurs while the participants are seated on low pillows, served by either the host or younger members of the temple or shrine. If a conversation is intended, the host is asked a question by the guest of honor. Long and illuminating discussions often developed in this form.

An especially memorable discussion took place when the Zen Master, Hisamatsu, whom we knew from Harvard, showed us the famous seven-hundred-year-old rock garden connected to his temple. The garden is surrounded by a wall of astonishing colors produced by nature over a period of about five hundred years. The ground is gravel, raked in an oceanic pattern, but most important are about fifteen rocks, ordered in groups of two, three, or more in perfect proportions of distance, height, and breadth. The chief priest of the temple and Mr. Hisamatsu and I fell into a discussion of over an hour about the question of whether the rock garden and the universe are identical (the Buddhist position) or non-identical but united by participation (my position). No amount of reading could replace such an experience.

We also had a special relation with the main temple of the largest Buddhist denomination, called the Jodo Shinshu (the True Sect of the Pure-Land Church, Eastern Branch). It represents the opposite pole of the Zen denominations. While Zen teaches the power of the individual to break through the state of unenlightenment to the state of enlightenment, Jodo Shinshu teaches the complete surrender to the compassion of the Buddha Power, embodied in its Amida or Kannon figure. The contrast between the two groups is also described as the difference between the "self-power" and the "other-power" faith. This is analogous to the contrast between Pelagius and Augustine and has profound consequences for religion as well as culture within Buddhism.

The archbishop of a large section of Jodo Shinshu is the father of a young man, Kosho Otani, who lived in our house in New York for a year while studying at Columbia University. As the eldest son, he is heir to the arch-episcopate and himself a priest. He arranged a long two- to three-hour discussion in the university which is under the archbishop's authority but is an acknowledged university of high standing. We discussed, among other things, the problem of the historical Gautama, called the Buddha (as the historical Jesus was called the Christ). The problem is almost completely neglected in the vast Buddhist literature and it is only now that some scholars are raising such questions. The majority take the traditional picture for granted and some groups, especially Zen, assert that the historical question is not of any religious concern.

We also had an elaborate Japanese dinner in their main temple. "Temple" designates a large complex of buildings including the houses of the priests, several devotional places, a treasure house, one or two pagodas, gardens, etc. All this is surrounded by an elaborate fence. One enters through immense gates of the highest architectural perfection. Kosho Otani's mother, a sister of the empress, was my table neighbor. She is a beautiful and noble lady, vivacious and outgoing despite the fact that we could communicate only through an interpreter: Richard DeMartino, an old pupil of mine, who acts as an interpreter for Hisamatsu and Dr. Suzuki in the United States and who is now living in Japan in Hisamatsu's temple complex. He attended most of my discussions with the Buddhists as an interpreter.

We were given beautiful reprints of some original sutras (holy scriptures) which are fundamental for the denomination. And we met twice again for several hours of discussion with a priest and a philosopher from the Otani group.

There were other discussions, especially with Buddhist philosophers, particularly philosophers of religion. Here I must mention our friend Professor Takeuchi of Kyoto University, who wrote an article in *Religion and Culture,* the *Festschrift* for my seventieth birthday, in which he contrasted my concept of "Being-Itself" with his concept of "Absolute Non-Being." He accompanied us on many trips and temple visits, arranging things for us and, in general, anticipating our wishes before we even had the chance to express them. He radiated something I don't know whether to call Buddhist *compassion* or Christian *agape.* I must also mention Professor Nishitani, a philosopher with a Buddhist speculative background but also with a deep understanding of both old and modern Western philosophy. His mind was incisive and logical. Professor Nishitani presided at a meeting of some twenty Buddhist scholars at which I was asked questions about various philosophical and theological problems. I, in turn, had the opportunity to ask them questions about Buddhism as a living religion, about the idolatrous distortion of symbols in popular Buddhism, about past or present reformations in their history, and about their interpretations of prayer. I have the feeling that Buddhism as a popular faith is an unsolved problem for most of them. Finally, I must mention a visit with Dr. Suzuki, whom I knew well from New York and Ascona, in one of the temples of Kamakura where he has his house and a rare library of Buddhist and Western literature. In spite of his ninety-two years, he was still able to have a long talk over an excellent Japanese dinner.

In a discussion with a Pure-Land Buddhist scholar the question arose as to the possibility of communion between persons. He made the statement, "If the individual self is a substance [in the sense of "standing upon itself"] then no communion is possible"; to which I replied that "only on this basis is communion—in contrast to realizing identity—possible."

The discussions with the Buddhists have shown me that their main points of difference with Christianity are always: the

Seated next to Paulus and Hannah is the sister of the Emperor of Japan

The Zen Master and Paulus

Suzuki and Paulus

Paulus and the Kamakura Buddha

different valuation placed on the individual, the meaning of history, interpersonal relations, religious and social reformation, and finitude and guilt. It is the contrast between the principle of identity and the principle of participation. It seems to me that, although the principles are mutually exclusive, the actual life of both Christianity, especially in its Protestant form, and Buddhism, especially in its monastic form, could receive elements from each other without losing their basic character.

This leads to the question of Japanese Christianity, a complex and serious problem. Quantitatively, Christianity is weak. Less than 1 percent of the population is Christian. Christianity's influence, however, is much greater than this statistic indicates. Its impact is mediated by outstanding individuals, by teachers in Christian schools, by professors in Christian universities (where, although fewer than 20 percent of the enrolled students are members of a Christian church, all are somehow under the influence of the spirit of the school), by the continuous exchanges with people who come from Christian cultures, and by the elements of Christian tradition which are being imported with the general Westernization of Japanese life. There are three Protestant groups in Japan: the largest is the United Church of Christ; the second consists of the Lutherans and Episcopalians who became independent again after having joined the United Church of Christ during the war; and third are the Non-Church Christians, a small group critical of all organized churches, who meet regularly in private houses for devotional purposes. With the Japanese Catholics—fewer in number than the Protestants—I had no contact.

It is an extraordinary feeling when one is in a pagan country for the first time and preaches in a tiny church to a small group of Christians. One feels nearer to early Christianity, and the question of missions becomes existential. All churches in such a situation have been founded by missionaries in the recent past and are mission churches by the mere fact of their existence. But here "missionary" does not mean what first comes to mind, namely a person who attempts to convert pagans to Christianity by a direct preaching approach. In Japan the missionaries use indirect methods and wait for those who come to them.

[105]

Secondly, it is not the active pagan religions—Buddhism, Shinto-ism, and the New Religions—which are the main object of the missionary's task, but the masses who are without a religious preference. Therefore, as I said in one of my lectures, Chris-tianity should not present itself as simply another religion, but as what it truly is, namely a message over and against all religions, Christianity included. In this respect, the problem of Christianity in both East and West is the same. And thirdly, this leads to the question, "On what theological basis is such preaching possible?" The predominant theology in Tokyo is "Barthian" (not Barth's), which corresponds to the fact that the predominant philosophy is analytic philosophy. In Kyoto, metaphysics in philosophy and a moderate liberalism in theology prevail. Two questions are important for the situation in Japan: whether or not a theology is able to give foundation to the distinction between the "Christian event" and the religious reception of that event in the Christian religion, and whether or not a theology is able to express the "Christian event" in concepts which can be received by a highly civilized nation in its own language.

This last question leads us to the fourth problem of Christianity in Japan, the problem of communication. There are fundamentalist groups who consider the language of the two Testaments the unique and exclusive language of revelation and who attempt to impose it on the Japanese people. The majority, however, realize that Christian churches have been using a language incomprehensible to the people among whom they live. They ask, "What language (language here means form of expression) is understandable to the Japanese?" If this is asked seriously, a fifth problem arises. For, is there one language only, or are there not at least two: the language of the highly educated, often influenced by Buddhist elements, and the language of the masses, who live on the level of a primitive Shintoism or a magically distorted Buddhism? And is there not in fact a third level, that of Confucian ethical traditions, and even a fourth, that of Western skeptical indifference? These levels do exist and the churches should be able to speak in the language of each of them. But to do so they must free themselves from the language in which Christianity was given to the missionaries, that is, of

American Methodism or Continental Lutheranism. If they cannot transcend their denominational heritage in the power of their Christianity, one cannot see how they will reach the hearts of the Japanese people. Quite a few Japanese Christian theologians are aware of this situation, among them my friend and translator, Dr. Ariga, and my former pupil Mrs. Chow, who is now a professor at the International Christian University in Tokyo. But the road is full of obstacles and demands a total rethinking of the role of Christianity in the Asiatic world.

I referred several times to Shintoism. Hannah and I visited the two main Shintoist shrines, the Meiji shrine in Tokyo and the Ise shrine in the south. The latter is the more sacred, the former the more important politically. We were guided by priests of the shrine on both visits and, in Tokyo, it was a quite solemn occasion. We were shown the water of purification and afterward entered the inner section of the shrine where we saw a colorful wedding. We were, of course, not admitted to the innermost part, which contains the sacred mirror and is reserved for the emperor. We were led to a teahouse in a garden adjoining the shrine where we had a ceremonial tea and a long discussion about the relation of the Shinto gods (kamis) to the universe they represent and about the way in which the Shinto believer can achieve salvation. In the course of the discussion, the High Priest admitted that the problems of sin and guilt were foreign to this thought. The religious function of Shinto pantheism (this word can be used here, but not with respect to Buddhism) seems to me a double one: to maintain both the memory of and reverence for the past generations in one's family and nation. In the Meiji shrine, the "spirit" of Emperor Meiji is "present." In this context, the word "spirit" does not mean "immortal soul," although this is often imagined in the act of devotion. Nor does it mean the Platonic essence of a being, although this is a possible philosophical interpretation. The word is perhaps closest to the Roman *manes* (e.g., of the emperors who also received sacrifices). When the Eisenhower visit was being planned, the question arose as to whether or not he should see the Meiji shrine. The Christian churches and some Buddhist groups were against it because they were afraid the visit might strengthen not

[107]

only Shintoism as such, but also the connection between church and state—a tie which had been radically cut by General MacArthur and the constitution he gave Japan.

Another side of the Shinto influence is in the relation of all classes of the Japanese people to nature. One of the most impressive things about the Ise shrine was its tremendous cryptomeria trees. The loss of several of them in the last typhoon had saddened everyone. And the teahouse garden of the Meiji shrine has the most beautiful water lilies and irises. We visited it on our own one Sunday morning and admired not only the exquisite design of the garden but also the pilgrim-like devotional attitude of the Japanese walking slowly beside the flower beds. On the desk at one of my first lectures was a crooked pine tree of about half my height—just as it would appear in a Japanese painting. Gardens and flower arrangements permeate every sector of Japanese life. In all this, Shinto influence is present. It is lived pantheism. But its religious power is limited. Thus, Buddhism had a comparatively easy entrance into Japanese life after the fifth century A.D. And just as it took on Chinese characteristics in China, Buddhism took on Japanese characteristics in Japan. But Buddhism brought something that Shintoism lacked: an answer to the problem of suffering and death. The entire situation is nicely symbolized by the fact that most Japanese are Buddhists as well as Shintoists. They go to the shrine for the wedding ceremony and the Buddhist priest for the funeral.

The comparative stagnation of Buddhism and Shintoism, especially among the lower classes, has given rise to a large group of so-called "New Religions." They have partly Buddhist, partly Shintoist backgrounds and are all more or less syncretic (uniting elements from different religions and religious levels). There are several reasons for the strong appeal of these "New Religions" to the masses. The most external one is the fact that the new constitution guarantees religious freedom. This freedom has been used by religious and pseudo-religious men to gather groups around themselves by claiming to have received a new revelation. And herein lies the second reason for their appeal, namely the desire for an immediate divine manifestation, which as such has unquestioned authority. In no case I saw was it the content of the revelation that was impressive. Rather, it was the way in which it was communicated.

Tendri, which existed before the new constitution concealed it as a Shinto sect, was the largest group I saw. It is centered around a simple peasant woman's experience of revelation. Her words now have canonic validity for three million enthusiastic followers.

We visited the community and temple they had constructed and were invited to a splendid dinner with the archbishop. The followers make astonishing sacrifices for the sect in terms of money, pilgrimages, and voluntary service. As a result it is very rich and possesses large buildings, schools, and a university as well as a museum and a library, both full of treasures in art and manuscripts. The sect has Shinto elements. There are magic dances and the followers express their veneration for the founder by daily bringing food to her spirit.

In Tokyo, we encountered another, basically Buddhist, "New Religion." It, too, has a large following ready for every sacrifice. So they are building one pink house after another (pink is their chosen color). Their new temple will be one of the largest buildings in Tokyo, with a cupola that seems to surpass even that of the Cathedral of St. Peter in Rome.

But what most interested me was their method of counseling. It is done in large halls where groups of from fifteen to twenty people, the majority of whom seem to be poor women, sit around in a circle asking questions about their personal problems and receiving answers from a leader, also usually a woman. Each day thousands are served in this manner. It is a kind of group counseling for people who have nowhere else to go with their troubles. And this is perhaps the key to the rapid growth of these sects, that the atomized individual finds in them a community in which his needs are taken seriously. The founder, a man of between fifty and sixty years of age and a former milk delivery man, had his inspiration about thirty years ago. He guided us through his "realm," in which he was greeted everywhere with reverence, and gave us the usual tea and gift.

In view of these "New Religions" both Christians and Buddhists must ask themselves serious questions, as they must in

[109]

the face of the vast amount of religious indifference. As a theologian, I asked myself, "What function does theology have in view of these successful eruptions of primitive religion in both the East and West?"

In giving my impressions of the political and religious spheres, I have pointed frequently to the realm of art. I wish now to speak directly about the arts in Japan. One's first impressions naturally come from Japanese architecture: from the design of the houses, temples, palaces, and shrines. One of the first things one realizes is that, in all these cases, wood is the only building material. A consequence of this is that there are very few buildings that are old with respect to their material. But there are many that are very old—dating from as early as the seventh century—with respect to their form. They were simply rebuilt after each fire in exactly the same manner. These buildings therefore show the style of the time in which they were conceived. Sometimes buildings are intentionally razed and rebuilt as is, for example, the Ise shrine every twenty years. Alongside the actual structure is an empty lot where the last shrine stood and the next will stand. The official idea behind it is that the holy shall not disintegrate.

Another general rule is that most Japanese houses have only one story. This makes them more adequate to the human measure and, at the same time, allows an intimate connection with nature (the Japanese house is usually oriented toward an often very small garden). Finally, the emptiness of the Japanese house, its minimal furniture (no chairs, very low tables, no beds, just mats and blankets. And no chests of drawers, only cupboards), and movable walls make it almost as flexible as a tent.

About the temple architecture I cannot say much beyond what is generally known. But one cannot admire enough the carpenter's art which has produced often very large temples, pagodas, and palaces without ever using a nail. The idea of perfection in the smallest pieces of work, which one can observe everywhere in Japan, has been realized in these buildings. This ideal is also manifest in the imperial palaces and villas. One of them, Katsura, has such perfect proportions that Walter Gropius, the famous modern architect, returned again and again to it during the months of his stay in Japan.

The Buddhist temples are filled with great works of sculpture, primarily of the Buddha, his trinity (the Buddha himself and his Powers of Mercy and Wisdom), the Bodhisattvas, the half-demonic Guardians of the Holy, great teachers and saints. The largest bronze figures of the Buddha are in Nara (one of the earliest capitals), and Kamakura (a later capital before Kyoto). The one in Kamakura dominates the landscape, overwhelming in its size and beauty. When we saw it, a few days after our arrival, I realized that for the next two months I would be living in its shadow—though more in a cultural than a religious sense. Hannah and I were almost always impressed by the holiness radiating from these sculptures. They represent not a god or gods but the Buddha Power, the spirit of awakening; of opening the mind's eye to truth about oneself, one's world, and that which is above both of them and is present in the Buddha Spirit.

On the subject of painting I can make only a few personal remarks. We were the guests of the director and founder of the Museum for Folk Arts. After a ceremonial tea, we discussed the influence of religion on artistic style. The director showed us several scroll paintings influenced by Zen Buddhism, the religion of "self-power," and others influenced by Shin Buddhism, the religion of "other-power." The comparison was quite illuminating. The Zen style has a strong tendency toward concentration or, to use Schelling's term, "essentialization." We had a fully developed Zen tea ceremony under "The Four Persimmons," a famous painting of this style. The fruits are painted in such a way that each of them represents "being-itself," which, for Buddhism, is "non-being." They are something, but their being is transcended toward absolute nothingness—beyond subject and object. Therefore, such paintings are usually done in various shades of black and white, in which color, so to speak, is negated. By contrast, the Shin type of Buddhism, the Amida religion with a belief in divine mercy reaching down to a suffering world, has produced a more colorful art: less reduced, less sharp-edged. It is hardly surprising that Confucianism, with its exclusive emphasis on social and political ethics, has contributed little to the visual arts. Without Mahayana Buddhism's invasion of the Far East, the great art of China and Japan would not exist.

In ceremonial acts, religious and aesthetic elements are

mixed. We attended two tea ceremonies in which the tea master prepared the ceremonial tea. Ordinarily, these acts are omitted as in all cases mentioned previously. The preparation for the tea ceremony is a long series of manipulations with the water, tea, cups, and tools necessary for the preparation of the perfect tea. It produces a mood of mutual belongingness among the participants and may be accompanied by either gay or serious conversation. We also saw a ceremony done in a restaurant before about a hundred people, which we felt to be a desecration. Unfortunately, this is the type destined for export. Even more unfortunately, such export is defended by some high ranking Zen people with the argument, which is so important for their own problems, that the good, even distorted, has some illuminating power. They do not acknowledge demonized symbols. "Buddism is not demonized," I was told.

We saw two ceremonial dances at the Ise shrine, one public, done by girls, and one performed especially for us by about twelve men. Before the public dance, a religious ceremony was held and a cup of sake given to every participant. After the two dances, we had a special meeting with the priests at which we received some of their sacramental food as a gift. Hannah saw a procession with the old costumes as they are commonly worn at the many local festivals (most of which we missed).

We attended three forms of classical Japanese theater (the fourth is still reserved for the emperor and his invited guests). The oldest and most ceremonial form is the No play. The performances take six hours and only male actors are used, even for the female roles. They enter in beautiful ancient-style costumes and the most important actors also wear masks, which are genuine works of art. The actors speak in specially trained voices, accompanied by music which has a limited tone scale and in which the rhythm-creating drum is quite important. The plots are based on old legendary and mythological stories. No was the form of the court and nobility, who often performed the No play themselves.

The second oldest form is the puppet theater, which was always open to the people. Three performers serve each puppet on the open stage: the main actor, whose face is uncovered, and two attendants who are veiled in black. The first of these moves

[112]

the head, upper body, right hand, eyelids, and lips of the puppet, while the two others move the left hand and legs. Ten years of training is necessary to do this to perfection. But even more important is the speaker who, sitting with the musicians and accompanied by music, verbally re-creates the role and mood of each character. After the performance, Hannah and I were invited backstage and shown the inner mechanism of the puppets and the way they are moved.

The third form, the Kabuki, is the most modern and has become the most popular. We spent almost six hours (including an intermission for dinner) attending one. Since it has been shown in America, I don't need to say much about it. It is more dramatic, more naturalistic, and less stylized than No, but it did not impress us as deeply as the latter.

All this, Japan's great past, reaches into but is no longer actual for the present. The younger Japanese feel estranged from the past and are looking for new ways. But they try to keep something of their tradition. This became clear to us after seeing several exhibitions of modern Japanese art. There is a tremendous struggle going on to depart from the old traditions without becoming imitators of modern Western styles in all their phases of development. Only rarely does one find someone who has to a certain degree solved this problem.

I will also say a few words about the landscape. Japan reminds me more of Europe than of America. The latter's large, monotonous plains are lacking and the landscape is extremely varied. We had the rare luck to see Mount Fuji twice for quite a time. All the postcards in the world cannot spoil the impression of divine greatness it gives. Mount Ashama, a smoking volcano at whose foot we lived during our five-day stay in Karuizawa, has the classical form of a volcano. The smaller mountains and hills reminded us of southern Germany. And we saw, for the first time, the cultivation of rice fields. Through an artful irrigation process, the fields are kept underwater for the greatest part of the year. The farmers work in them either barefoot or in high boots. We also saw tea and mulberry plants. And we took a boat trip through two beautiful bays with many islands where cultured pearls and oysters are cultivated. The ocean is everywhere near.

Much has been written about the major cities, especially the

[*113*]

two in which we lived—Tokyo and Kyoto. Kyoto, Nara, and one other city were saved from the bombing through the advice of an American committee of art experts. The Japanese speak gratefully about this fact which has become almost legendary. The large-scale destruction of Tokyo, its rapid and unplanned reconstruction and the immense growth of the world's largest city, have given it the character of a city with many centers. Each of these centers has a railway station around which the business and shopping streets are situated. Between the centers are the residential districts. There is, however, one universal center near the large island on which lies the imperial palace. (The palace, however, is neither visible from the city nor open to the public. It lies concealed in a vast park.)

Beautiful are the views of Tokyo's narrow streets with shops, restaurants, bars, teahouses, etc., especially in the evening, when they all turn on their colorful neon signs written in picture-like Japanese letters. The traffic is immense, the masses of human beings overwhelming and sometimes frightening. Yoshivara, the so-called red-light district, has been abolished, though its streets, with their bars and nightclubs, still show their former function. Prostitution is forbidden but, of course, not suppressed. Prostitution, however, must be distinguished from the institution of geishas, who are social entertainers for individuals or groups, well organized according to a kind of hierarchy and local distinctions, very expensive, often unattainable, maintaining a dying tradition in which beauty and tragedy are mixed. (This we gathered from friends who organized and shared our own geisha party.)

After three weeks in Tokyo we took a six-hour train ride to Kyoto. Whoever speaks of Kyoto becomes enthusiastic. It can be compared with Florence both for its beautiful landscape and as a repository of art treasures. And, like old Florence, it is also a center of intellectual life which is concentrated there and at the other universities such as Doshisha, Otani, etc. The three weeks in Kyoto were the most intensive of my stay in Japan and indeed one of the most intensive periods of my life. This was true with respect to work, discussions, and sightseeing (including two days for Nara and another two for the Ise shrine). The charm of this ancient capital, with its innumerable temples and several palaces and imperial villas, is great and the things to discover inexhaustible.

For a long time I was undecided whether or not the trip to Japan was justified, especially at my age and with the heavy obligations to my other work. Any doubt in this respect has been removed by the actual experience. I cannot formulate what it has meant before all the impressions have settled down in me; and even then, others will probably notice the influence of Japan on me more than I myself will. But I know that something has happened. From now on, no Western provincialism of which I am aware will be tolerated by me in my thought or in my work. I am deeply grateful to my Japanese friends, who worked for such a long time to make my trip and this insight possible. I can tell them that I have learned to love Japan and her people.

HANNAH WRITES

Soon after our arrival in Tokyo, we got in touch with German friends there, at the invitation of one of our truly close friends from Washington who had also emigrated from Hitler's Germany. After dinner, they took us to our first Japanese bar, where we indulged in the famous Japanese drink, sake, served in tiny cups. Paulus, in high spirits, disregarded all our well-meant warnings and drank about twenty-one thimblefuls of the delightfully warming and stimulating liquid.

When it was time to leave, he found he could not step on his swollen foot and toe—an unexpected recurrence of gout. With our friends' help, and his own tremendous will power, despite miserable pain, we managed to get him to the Japanese house of Eugene L., our host for our first few days in Japan. A German, Dr. Eitel, who had known Paulus through his work as well as reports from mutual friends, was called. And so, as had happened earlier in Israel, a German doctor in Japan quickly relieved Paulus's pain with medication.

Eugene, seeing that Paulus looked as if he would be in bed for at least one or two days, conferred with the Japanese

[115]

committee that had arranged the lectures. Together they decided to place an ad in one of the Japanese newspapers to inform the audience that Dr. Tillich's lecture would be postponed. The next morning Eugene appeared, confessing in utter embarrassment that, through a mistaken sign in the complicated Japanese language, the newspaper had declared Paulus dead, instead of simply too ill to lecture. To the great relief of both Eugene and the editor, Paulus and I took the confusion as mere confusion and laughed off the error. Very quickly, Paulus—with a bandaged foot in a shoe cut open to enable him to get his swollen foot into it, under medication, and trying to stick to a diet—found himself lecturing again.

At the end of the lectures in Tokyo, Dr. Eitel invited us for a Japanese dinner—fish with a red sweet-and-sour sauce. Afterward he took us to his very German home and the best of all German wines.

·

The Liftons took us to a nightclub featuring an exotic striptease. Slim-hipped, small-breasted girls with ivory skin go through the motions of our sensuously bobbing American burlesque routine. We sit in the first row of tables around the circular stage. Two of the Japanese beauties come close to the two men and one of the black-haired girls touches Paulus's face with her small breasts.

We go on to a Japanese dance hall where there are 350 kimono-clad Japanese girls, shoulders bare, skirts split to show the legs to the knees and beyond.

·

I insist on going to a horse race during one of Paulus's lectures, but wind up at the Sumo wrestling. Under an enormous tent on a raised platform encircled by countless rows of seats, large, muscular Japanese with bare torsos stand in deadly embrace, seemingly without moving. It is an extraordinary feat of balance between the two fighting men. Unexpectedly, they break into motion, one throwing his adversary to the ground with a single, powerful thrust. I find it chilling to watch the seesaw of balance in these strained musclemen. My Japanese friends had not approved of my going off on a nontheological adventure.

[116]

When I returned to the International House where we were now staying, I glimpsed on a television screen in the lobby what I am sure was the end of a fight I had left reluctantly. It seems to be a great Japanese pastime.

•

I envision our Japanese friends from the International House, riding with Paulus and me in the comfortable, fast electric train between Tokyo and Kyoto. We eye the miniature landscape, rice fields, green porcupines of tea plants, a Mediterranean-blue ocean. Leaving the ocean, the rails plunge our train into the mountains, just as on Italy's Riviera. We get a glimpse of Fujiyama with its symmetrical slopes, the most striking volcano I have ever seen. For the Japanese, seeing Fujiyama brings happiness.

I seemed to live in Japan by the principles of aesthetics. We saw so much. Experts from several university faculties accompanied us on our trips, to show us the beauty of their works of art—architectural, sculptural, and painted. Without the medium of language, we participated through empathy in their endeavor to show us beauty. One of the professors of art history might touch a sculpture, to make me feel spontaneously what he wished to convey. The sensitivity of our Japanese friends to us and our delight in deciphering their silent communication was one of the enchantments of this trip to strange shores. There seemed to be a kind of osmosis between us.

Dick DeMartino was with us as an interpreter, when the Zen Master Hisamatsu invited us to his temple to see the dragon in the ceiling of the Meditation Hall. I experienced the dragon as a joyful dragon, which gave me a sense of triumphant power. "When the fish rises above the water, he becomes a dragon, mastering the waves." Did Hisamatsu say it to me?

After the dragon, Paulus, our American theologian of German descent, and I went to the Zen Master's house for dinner. We took him the Japanese candies that seem too sweet for our tongues, to eat with the harsh and bitter green Japanese tea during a tea ceremony. I listen to their conversation. Hisamatsu wishes to spread the ceremony through the Zen centers in both Japan and the United States, to influence personally, socially, and politically. Paulus regrets it; he feels it would destroy the intimacy and delicacy of the ritual.

The Zen Master, Paulus, and I walk to the famous Garden of Royan-ji, the rock garden with the centuries-old wall sheltering its far side. The men sit and talk. I dream along with them and apart from them, visualizing an old wall with little green moss pillows between its cracks, where I played as a child. It was near our house, protecting a section of the plaza in front of our church. There I would pick up stones and make a garden of them, combing the dusty soil before the wall with my fingers.

John D. Rockefeller III, a young giant, walks into our luxurious hotel. He partakes of a meal, he talks about his mother, and looks with amused scorn at us wine-drinking, cigarette-smoking sybarites. He lived with a Japanese working family and, except for a super-sized bed, participated in their style of living.

We are invited to the Ise shrine. Two priests—one with a small underlip and the other with a head that looks as if it had been clapped between two boards—walk with us across a bridge of trees. Colorful bantam roosters and hens run in the road. We stop before a fence with a closed entrance; one of the priests kneels, both clap their hands. We move on to another spot, where we are permitted to see the room where the mirror is installed that only the emperor or his messenger may look into. Prayers and dances for us, shrill music, penetrating drums, shaman-like headdresses, fertility rites, and tree worship, which we can happily participate in, walking along the aisles of tall cryptomeria trees and admiring divine old giants standing in lonely grandeur. We share in a communion luncheon, with sake, polyps, fish, and seaweed. The priest with the flat face, who had called for us, returns us to our hotel, an hour and a half in a good Buick through torrential rain along a country road.

We visit the artificially seeded oyster beds in a dreamy bay . . . green islands, wooded mountains. Our friend Takeuchi helps me buy a lovely string of pearls brought from the oyster beds by lithe pearl fisherettes, and strung right there on the pier.

Abe, a Japanese friend who is a professor, takes me to the temple where I meet a monk who guides me into the Meditation Hall, to sit za-zen. None of the monks was meditating at the time. Abe and the monk stay nearby. From a small shrine the Buddha of wisdom looks on. I hear water dripping, the noises of a loudspeaker and of children. Laid out before me are the dark squares of the polished floor. The noises diminish, silence enfolds me, the last sounds to become mute are drops of falling water. I go away . . . until the monk rings a bell, recalling me. He shows me how to sit straighter, chest out, chin close to the neck, nose in the same plane as the navel, left hand under right hand, thumbs together in a triangle. I meditate again for twenty minutes. He advises, "Count your breaths from one to ten until you lose counting." I do so. I show the monk my way of Yoga breathing.

I am introduced to the Reverend Zenkei Shibayama. We talk through an interpreter (was it Abe again, the friendly spirit of my meditation adventure?). I ask about dangers in meditation. We talk about Zen and Yoga. Zen, after reaching Samadhi, returns to the duality of life. One of my problems is what to exclude and what to include. His advice is gentle: "Don't try too hard."

Paulus preaches in a Christian church in Japan. The atmosphere and people seem provincial to me. Paulus's sermon comes as a voice from another world.

I find in my sketchy diary, where I mostly try to follow Paulus's lectures, a jumble of words and syllables that follow the Japanese translation of the sermon without understanding. I slip from English into Japanese for a whole page. Either I must have considered it excruciatingly funny, or perhaps it made sense to me if I were following with some sort of empathy. I ended the language confusion by slipping again into English sentences, where Paulus was talking about the Logos and the question of the historical Jesus.

A friend of ours tells me that, during a lecture by Professor Nishitani at Kyoto University, the conversation touched on a passage of the New Testament, where St. Paul says: "And when I pray, it is not I who am praying but God prays within me." It was phrased to mean that in my prayer, God, as well as I, is praying. Nishitani put a question to Paul Tillich that was essentially a Koan, namely, "Who is praying, then?" Nishitani meant to point with this question to a realm that has greater depth than the "as well as." A peculiar silence arose after the question, and in this silence Paul Tillich bowed unexpectedly and in grand simplicity, placing the palms of his hands together and touching the tips of his fingers to his forehead, remaining for a short time concentrated in this gesture. The friend reports that he glanced at Nishitani, whose face was lit from within in a loving smile, which disappeared only when Paul Tillich, awakening from his absorption, nodded to Nishitani, who responded with an almost imperceptible nod. The whole scene took place in a few seconds and united Paul Tillich with everything Zen represented to our friend, who at that time was studying Zen with two masters. Paul Tillich could not have answered the question in a more genuine way than by this silent, true testimony. This experience, our friend said, has an everlasting presence for him. It might have happened yesterday, or it could happen any time in the future.

India and Southeast Asia, 1966

HANNAH ALONE

I disengaged myself from my known companion. He had been offended by the cosmic loneliness of the airplane rushing through nothingness between heaven and earth, more isolated than a star. Loosened up by a drink or two, he had begun talking to the stranger in the seat next to him.

There were crowds on the airfield and in the coming and departing planes. A wall of dark faces, brown eyes staring, heads immobile, stood like carvings on a ribboned frieze. They stared without focal point, looking inward at some private image of our emergence. I saw a Brahmin, surrounded by friends and hangers-on, all laughing eagerly at his sarcastic observations. Disembodying the event of our arrival, he condemned it to nonexistence with his lashing tongue.

To the Western eye, the Indians looked ridiculous in the early morning. The men wore turbans or simple pieces of cloth wrapped around their heads against the cold. Slung under their chins and tied in a bow at the top of their heads, the cloth made them look like long-eared rabbits. Some wore Western tweed or Nehru jackets, or a long shirt that flapped over their muslin dhotis, letting the other transparent cloth swish around their hairy legs. When in a hurry they would hitch the dhotis up to reveal ankles, calves, and feet very often covered in heavy, newly polished black or brown shoes.

An Oriental street view. Wealthy sections with modern but cheaply constructed houses. An open-air laundry surrounded by a low wall. The women beat their wash mercilessly against the cement sides of rectangular troughs. They worked rhythmically together in a kind of raw fury.

The Hanging Gardens is a friendly park atop a reservoir. Cricket playing fields and trees.

Vultures hang in the trees at the Parsi towers of silence waiting to devour the corpses of the faithful.

A Hindu temple. The goddess of wealth, a pale alabaster doll decorated with flowers, peers out of black-rimmed eyes. Kneeling Indians, standing Indians. Some form swastikas of rice on a stone slab. Others smear the image of the goddess with saffron colors. Indian women wearing the sign of Siva, a red dot on the forehead. My woman guide says quickly: "It is the fashion now."

An hour-and-a-half boat ride through the harbor, skirting little islands, passing the big ships from the ocean. A stiff breeze blows out of a cloudless sky. I am scared. At last, a small wooden dock. The tide is out and trees are growing in the now shallow water, some of the few green-leafed trees anywhere that grow in salt water.

One hundred and twenty-five steps rise before us, temple steep. Four men carried my guide and me up the stairs. It went smoothly, with only one stop before we reached the entrance of the cave. During the monsoon season that entrance is often flooded and unreachable, as it is of course whenever the tide is in.

The three-faced Siva cut out of the brown stone of the hillside was a shock. It seemed so much more incredible in its sculptural reality than it had in the pages of my art book, described as the Trimurti of Elephantia. The three-faced Siva— the destroyer on the left, the feminine aspect on the right, Jupiter-Siva in the center, the whole more than eight feet high, with the left side of the body, as well as the face, shown as male, the right side as female. And all done with such naturalness. My first encounter with phallic representation of the god—the lingam in the curve of the yoni.

[122]

Aurangabad

Houses in Aurangabad flank its one main street, single-story wooden houses with built-in balcony niches. Within, business as well as family living all takes place in one undivided area. Beyond the main street lie mud and straw-thatched huts.

The caves of Ajanta are laid out in the shape of a crescent moon. From one point you can see all entrances, their frontal courts hollowed out of the hillside. The builders had brought the emptiness of space into the density of the hillside. They had put a layer of cow dung and clay on the cave walls when it was first dug out and created paintings with the colors provided by the earth itself. They had put a mirror at the mouth of the cave so they could see what they were painting. We had to carry light bulbs on long cords to see where we were going. Some of the painted surfaces are badly damaged and are hard to see. However, the feminine and masculine dignity, the grace of a bent head, the noble humility of the curve of a neck and full breasts, the delicacy of slender hands were seductive.

The sky above Ajanta was clear, and many Indians were coming and going among the sanctuaries. I remember one beautiful girl with earrings, nose ring, and ankle rings and bracelets, all glittering and tittering together. In a wild combination of skirt, blouse, and shawl, dark-haired and cherry-eyed, she hid her face against one of the pillars of the court.

In Ellora, the Kailasa Cave 16 is a temple cut out of the mountain. The Hindus had carved an entire stone cliff, working from the top to peel out the ivory-like images in honor of Siva, the mountain-dwelling god. The walls tell his story, a big, wonderful picture book of his deeds. The temple is a sculptured shrine. There is not much inside.

Ellora is the playground for Hindus, Buddhists, and Jains. Monks and worshipers had left Ajanta for Ellora centuries ago. They had dug classrooms, living quarters, and shrines from these new hills, from where they could watch the sunset at the entrances of their cells. In some caves, Buddhist and Hindu images were joined, the smiling Buddha contemplating in a cave dedicated to a Hindu saint, or Siva with Parvati, his beautiful wife. Siva dancing the dance of destruction, the lingam, the bull, Durga, the negative aspect of the mother goddess, Vishnu and his wife, Lakschmi—they are all there together.

Udaipur

Hill country, cool blue skies. We cross in barges to a white dream palace in an artificial lake. Mogul architecture, lace stone filigree in inner courts, marble floors, marble arches, and inlaid marble walls, the whole splendor icy-cold after sunset. Waiters with turbans and godlike faces . . . toilet paper becomes soft and pink . . . American and maharajah civilization mix . . . pigeons coo in the ornaments of outer walls. Udaipur, land of princes, abode of kings descended from the heroes of the Ramayana and Mahabbarata. Women's quarters with marble-laced peekaboo windows, a garden on the palace roof, marble arcades, a room with peacock mosaics spreading multicolored tails. Fountains in gold and shimmering mosaic.

Inserted in one wall are colored pieces of glass the size of the palm of one's hand. The women would look through a smoky, lavender-colored pane if they were in the mood to see the moon. To see the monsoon, they would turn to a burnt-green pane, and if they wished to feel the terror of coming things or remember past horrors, they looked through a cloudy blue fragment. Clear-cut arches and cloverleaf shapes repeat themselves through seemingly endless corridors.

It is told that when the Ramayana had to flee his enemies, he swore he would not eat from his gold and silver dishes until he regained his empire. And when it was lost for good, he put a banana leaf on his gold and silver plate before dining, and since he had promised not to sleep in his gold and silver bed, he put straw under his bed.

The kings of Europe created and lived in high splendor, but probably only those of France managed to equal the blinding brilliance of a maharajah's empire. The princely attempt to imitate the light of the moon and the stars and the sun is the same as the desire of the poor for gold-paper glitter, for imitation precious stones set into necklaces aping the shape of ancient designs in gold and diamonds, for earrings and bracelets in new cheap materials—plastic bubbles and rhinestone iridescence from the five-and-dime stores. What fun for a low-salaried shopgirl to jump the threshold labeled "genuine" and own a necklace à la Nefertiti. But of course, the desire of the princes of this world has been to express in their buildings and appurtenances that brilliance derived from ancestral majesty and their own inner, spiritual splendor.

There were no representations of the human being in the mogul palaces. The clear-cut arches and the decorative patterns of the breezy galleries and balconies simply please the eye. Large halls for the people to kneel before the maharajah, but no portrayal of the human figure. The maharajah would be the one isolated human inhabitant of his wide palace. No embracing portrayal on the walls to show him how it is done. Only the reflection of his lonely power in the mirror to remind him of the ambiguities of life.

On the way to the temple of Vishnu through the narrow streets lined with stone houses, we met a wedding party, the bridegroom for one day in the costume of Krishna, strutting in the splendor of his outfit.

Indira Gandhi was speaking in Udaipur. The guide drove me to the field in great excitement. We went through the enclosure to the point where men and women separated. The usher, a tiny girl with a flower on her dress, guided me to the women's section. We sat down on blankets and rugs the guards had spread on the dusty ground. I was surrounded by children filled with gentle, chattering curiosity. Some touched my patterned stockings, some wanted my address, one boy shouted, demanding it. That was the strange thing about these gentle, apathetic Indians: they could burst out in violent gestures, their gentle faces suddenly arrogant in hostility—the waiters, the guides, the beggars whining and pushing, so insistent that they lost their claim to charity. I wondered about their eruptions of irritation when I read that the

[125]

cow-obsessed people in Puri and Bhubaneswar had bashed in Indira Gandhi's nose in a fit of mass hysteria, never having been permitted to become aware of their underlying genuine anger and frustration. But they all came to the meeting. Most of them probably could not read; nevertheless, they could listen. They could even decide whom to cast their ballots for. They were eager; they had become involved.

From the maharajah's palace, we took a motorboat to an island with a decaying palace of the seventeenth century. Crocodiles—two lazy beasts on a rock in the water glide into the lake ... cormorants ... vultures in trees, lethargically flapping their wings, waiting. We are waiting for the green parrots to flit over the lake (artificial—maharajah style), winging out of the sky, separating and shooting away from us in all directions. They arrive every evening at sunset, twittering madly, green birds with red beaks, hanging in the broad-leafed banyan trees like leaves themselves, chirping, gossiping.

When the tourists come en masse to the remodeled palace with its nightclubs and swimming pool, the green birds will leave. The tourists will do the gossiping and twittering. Tonight there were only a dozen or so, listening peacefully, beaming with pleasure, walking back leisurely to the boat.

I overheard two sweet old ladies actually in tennis shoes chirping to each other while we were waiting for the green parrots. "Now, what do you think? Let's find out about the crocodiles and the amorous couples on the temples and we will have a little project going."

Jaipur

I liked best the observatory—built of stone and metal in a large, walled-in compound. The most perfect architectural contraptions and nonobjective art, circular cavities, circular copper plates fastened to slabs of rectangular marble, on which latitude and longitude were marked. It reminded me of some outdoor sculpture in a sunken garden on the New Haven campus. I gave up trying to understand and wished I could take the assembly of this pure, geometrical cosmos home to my garden in East Hampton.

In the immediacy of tourist life you are on a globe accelerated in its turning, leaping from country to country in the terrifying loneliness of a pressure chamber, losing hours, gaining hours, utterly confused in your physical habits. You must have a thousand ears, a thousand eyes, and as many hands, to see, to hear, to touch. Not reading or thinking about it all, nor comparing statistics, nor wishing to improve, not even wishing to praise ... just being there is the goal. And if the image of the Buddha is precious enough, if the face of the native daughter or son awakens you enough, you may be transformed by an instantaneous experience, taking it into the center of your heart.

The hotel room had a high ceiling. It was 21 by 14 feet with wood paneling, an electric fireplace, a huge bathroom. I had seen a notice that one could apply for a massage. I did.

After dinner a man appeared. He wore a mustache, was small, ugly, and bald. I lay down on the mattress he had arranged in front of the fireplace, surrounded by pillows with elephant patterns. He was a superb masseur and I believe it was thanks to him that I was able to enjoy the Taj Mahal as I did the next morning.

When he was nearly finished, he commenced to talk. It sounded like gibberish but at last I caught on, I think: through massage, I could acquire firm, young, balloon-like breasts again. "I do not want to be loved any more, I am glad I am no longer young," I exclaimed. He muttered a discouraged, "Ah so."

Taj Mahal

Never read about the Taj Mahal unless you have seen it, unless you have come by air or water, or by foot, your heart filled with the certainty that you have to touch, that there is something on the other side of the Pacific which abolishes heaviness forever, which transforms stone into spheres lighter

[127]

than dandelions gone to seed. It is less than a monument, it is nothing but a smile, nothing but the shadow of a vision of a white cloud.

Not that it does not belong to our world. The old watchman who wanted to light my way with his flashlight let his light beam fall on the tricky entrance step. "It might be helpful," he said. Or the students walking briskly and the young couples uncertain of their fate under the star of the Taj Mahal—they were all real.

Delhi

I fell in love with the plain of India, with its crowns of trees, its haze over the vast horizon, its gray sky on a winter morning. The city smelled of coal. I took snapshots from the sumptuous balconies of the red fort overlooking the Jumna River. A human being, tiny against the vast sandy stretch along the sluggish Jumna, raised his hands to us.

After passing the power-conscious buildings representative of the former British Empire, I came through a tree-sheltered street to the gracefully understated American embassy. I spoke to the secretary at the desk, which had no pretensions. A call to the ambassador's office. Within minutes a personal secretary was arranging a date. The politeness of kings. My guide in Puri later said of Mr. Bowles, "The ambassador is a saint. And the ambassador's wife wears her sari with the grace of a noble Indian woman."

I arrived too late at the presidential reception after the Republican parade to see Indira Gandhi's entrance. By squeezing in among Indian nobles with their proud, intelligent faces, I saw the president of India arrive. Trumpets sounded as he walked in, clothed in white, under a canopy, red-uniformed guards surrounding him. The president, his hands folded in the Indian manner, frail and saintly with his remarkable philosopher's face under the baldachin of worldly power, looking down at his own heavily shod feet with an absent smile.

I joined the receiving line. Indira Gandhi sat on the president's left. In a low voice I said to her, "I am a friend of

Dorothy Norman. She sends her greetings." Her face came alive in quick response. "Delighted." I bent before President Ramakrishna, whom my husband had known as a philosopher.

I had seen Indira Gandhi before the parade, a small lonely figure riding along the parade route in a jeep, like a parade marshal. No cheering then, but flower petals rained down on us from airplanes.

Dalhousie

Off to Pathankot at 5:30 in the morning. The moon was full when we left New Delhi. It was cold throughout the plain of India.

I hired a car for the drive to the foothills of the Himalayas to see the Dalai Lama. My driver, a Pakistani, had brought some vegetables. I ate soup and rice, bread and tea in the evening. My driver ordered my bedding taken into the government bungalow and put on a bedstead, supervising, never touching anything. Indians came in to perform several tasks—bringing water and tea, cooking food. When they were given tips, they put the money to their foreheads, departing. I had one towel for the trip, which I unwittingly messed up the first morning, sometimes a portable toilet, but always plenty of hot water.

The first glance at the snow peaks of the Himalayas after endless turns on a one-way road. On our arrival in Dalhousie, the Pakistani moved himself and me to the Dalhousie Club when he discovered that the government bungalow had neither heat nor food. There I had a coal-burning fireplace and a tiny electric stove in my room. From the veranda on the first floor of the hotel one could see the Himalayas.

Two Indian gentlemen who were bank officials on holiday took me for a walk. They had prepared for the walk with great care, and looked like rabbits, shawls tied around their ears with the knots on top and the shawl ends sticking out. Along the way they introduced me to a friend, who in turn introduced me to a young Tibetan professor in rust-red Tibetan garb.

I had expressed the wish to walk to a Tibetan monastery. The three other gentlemen withdrew and the Tibetan walked with me to the monastery along a steep pathway, the towering mountains on our left raking the sky with their white clarity.

We had to bend low to enter the abbot's quarters. He sat on a couch covered with Tibetan rugs. A boy stood beside him. I sat facing him, a monk and my professor crowded the entrance. I gave the monk money for the monastery. I talked with the abbot through an interpreter. I felt tears come into my eyes, speaking of Paulus. The abbot wiped a tear from his eyes as he listened. He then took a white shawl from a cupboard and laid it over my outstretched hands.

When my Tibetan guide and I slithered back down the mountains, Tibetans came toward us with folded hands, and one put out his tongue in the age-old Tibetan greeting I had read about, which made me very happy. It moved me very much to see the first Tibetan faces over their monk's cowls. The monks and nuns dress in burnt ocher, working women in black. I had brought my mink stole but it was much too warm to wear it. My companion carried it for me and some of the Tibetan women came close to touch the fur, smiling and laughing with great good nature.

I had forgotten the name of my hotel, but we found it, along with a worried Pakistani and a cup of coffee for the professor, before he departed.

The Dalai Lama

About a mile from the Dalai Lama's residence, the trees looked holy. The Pakistani stopped the car. We found ourselves some hundred steps away from a whitish, fluttering human figure. The Pakistani pointed out a fat monkey and a small one, jumping from branch to branch in the trees on the slope below us. We went back to the car. As we drove past the white figure, it turned out to be a large dark rock with a wide cleft that was white inside. I saw it as a guardian watching the Dalai Lama's residence.

When the interpreter brought me to the Dalai Lama's residence, the Dalai Lama was standing on the terrace in his brownish-red monk's garb, one arm exposed, wrists together, hands opened toward me like an opening flower. I forgot everything in the way of etiquette. I fell into those open hands with mine. He took my arm and guided me into a room. He sat on the center sofa with me on his right.

He was slender; his bare arm had a vaccination mark. He used his hands often and he bent his head forward. He touched his strong dark eyebrows with his fingers. His intelligent face, eyes sparkling with life—he was altogether present. He was His Holiness the Dalai Lama. Our eyes joined. To be in his emanation was to be in a transparent golden shell. We all smiled. Even the cat coming toward us had laughter in her eyes, jumping, adoring the Dalai Lama, not because he was exalted but because of the radiance of his being.

We talked of the difference between meditation and concentration. I told him about "the tree" and my Japanese meditation. "So you want the light," he said. At first I did not understand. Now, I think I do. He made his point about my tree experience, using a table as an example. "You can, through meditation, dissolve an object into its atoms, and then it is not there." He said that the mind can leave the five senses behind.

We talked about the I-consciousness. He showed me relevant passages in his book. I told the story about the Zen Master saying of my husband, "He still makes the distinction between good and evil." At one point the translator was hard put to translate and remarked that for this kind of conversation the monks were usually present. We all laughed because it was clear they had expected a more commonplace conversation.

Speaking English slowed the discussion. The Dalai Lama threw in an occasional Tibetan word, waiting impatiently for the interpreter to translate. He was so full of the zest for life. We came to "the void," to "emptiness." "After you come through the void, you can distinguish." He got up and took me from the dark room onto the sunlit veranda, ordering coffee, saying, "Americans like coffee," and drinking his with relish.

He returned to the problem of illusion. He gave the example

[131]

of the snake and the rope. "It is a problem of fear. If we believe firmly, we see only the rope. The snake, the fear, will disappear. It is a question of illusion and delusion. The snake is not there if you do not intend to see it. It is all in your mind, but it has to be acted out. To return to the problem of the table: the goal is to see it and dissolve it and to revisualize it at any time." The problem of meditation: "to consider it [the object] from all sides and eventually dissolve it into atoms."

At one point in our conversation, I gave the Dalai Lama some of the ashes of my husband. He took one piece of bone out of the blue and gold enamel box I had bought in Florence, near the Ponte Vecchio. He smiled. He said, "When the person dies, the bones are nobody's. They do not belong to anybody. That is why the Tantric people make trumpets of bones and wear them as bracelets." He spoke to his companions in Tibetan, then said to me, "When I have time, I will pray for it." The Dalai Lama took the burden of my husband's ashes from me, the burden of those aspects of his life in our life that I had not been able to take into the silence of my heart and dissolve by love.

I had to take my leave. He took my hand and guided me out. He held my hand and I put my cheek against it. He said, "Since you are such a good Tibetan, I will give you a white shawl." He placed the shawl in my outstretched hand. "No," he said, "this is the way." And he put it around my neck. "What is it a sign of?" "For friendship and good luck." He bade me good-by, standing at the threshold of his house.

That night I dreamed that someone was choking me. I was in the grip of my own elbow, which I had wound too tightly around my neck. I prayed in my dream-sorrow: "Our Father, which art in Heaven." I prayed in German—I must have been among German-speaking people in my dream. I awakened with my prayer. The nightmare was gone.

Several days later, on the plane, I experienced a great shock. I was all in one piece and aware of it. My own being—my bones and flesh, eyes, ears, mouth, and my digestive system. It was all there and it was mine. My physical reactions had been haphazardly piecemeal, never as a unity. Now I was, all by myself, all in one piece and knowing it. I was scared.

On returning from the visit with the Dalai Lama, from the

car I observed that the animals were like people: I could see the enjoyment of buffaloes pulling their vehicles, I could see their pride in a good master, their willingness.

I saw many things on the road returning from Dalhousie: grass hoarded in the branches of trees for an emergency feeding of cattle; an old man having stones weighed so he could take them home and tell the weight of other things.

The following day, the Pakistani, in a burst of enthusiasm, made a detour to Chandigarh, the modern city designed by Le Corbusier. His delight in this modern city, in decent living quarters, was infectious. India's poverty-infested people, sharing mud huts with their animals, were challenged. Thant, the Pakistani emigrant, looked with hungry eyes at the splendor. He raced the car through the streets, I using up my last film. To Western eyes, it seemed not lived in, uncomfortably spread out between wide dusty streets, with hardly a moving vehicle. The stalls in the market did have the appearance of cleanliness and life, but the hotel was built of cheap materials and was run-down. It offended.

Khajuraho

The countryside is misty in the morning. I walk slowly, pleasuring it, from the village well where water was being hoisted, to the banyan tree with snakelike roots, to the shacks with red-tiled roofs. Men were soaping themselves along the steps to the river, women washing clothes in another spot. Desert climate— cold in the morning and evening, hot at noon.

The temple is a mountain for the gods, with creatures of the earth and heavens sculptured around the outside walls. Slowly, with the help of my guide, I discovered the elephants, the dancers, the kings, the processions of people, and love-making couples. I had no film left for the king putting his hand nonchalantly on the shoulder of his elected, while she looked up to him inflamed.

A boy shows me four stone elephants and a big red lingam painted with garlands of white. Money for the yoni before the lingam, money for the elephant. All four elephants are washed clean, dripping. I walk on through several shrines. Sculptures of Buddhas take me into their mood of meditative detachment. Neither the dripping water nor the whistle of the wind penetrates the quiet of the hour.

In one of the shrines, sparsely decorated and painted white, I surprise a voluptuous Hindu woman in a sari, scrambling down from a large lingam, her skirts flying. A man and a child stand by. The lingam is of marble and as highly polished from touch as the toe of St. Peter at the cathedral in Rome.

To me, the temples of Khajuraho were water buffaloes, lying in the river, in the canals, in the pools and puddles in the afternoon hour. On the night of a full moon they might all decide to shuffle off over the plain to another watering place and, dunking with a hissing sigh while the water sprays in fountains, come up dripping and shining—all the mithuna couples, the beasts and warriors and dancing girls drunk with glittering wetness.

Bhubaneswar

Back to the government hotel. It is still dirty, straw on the seats in the lobby, hens and dogs running in and out. The black birds of sunset are flying and cawing, not only in Calcutta but here as well. To watch the sun set, I venture out on the unkempt lawn within the compound of the government pavilion. People on bicycles are making their way past the modern houses that line the street. The scorched plain of India is spreading. Back in the hotel, people are scurrying about, mostly dirty, with an occasional flash of a white muslin dhoti, accomplishing nothing. Apathy in the air, and aimless movement.

The manager was barely polite next morning. I asked for a chair in the shade of the veranda before the hotel. He called a boy, then left me his own. I went back to my room to pack. The heat had become atrocious. The dirt was starting to smell, the toilet stank. I was disgusted.

Puri

Puri, like Italy's Paestum, is close to the sea. Puri on the Bay of Bengal, blue and smooth. As I arrived at the waterfront, just a minute from my clean hotel, dark-skinned fishermen were pulling in their nets. It would have taken two of the fish in their catch to fill the palm of my hand. The fishermen were sad. "No big fish." Could they eat them? "Yes, but they have so many bones." Brown boys offered me snakeskins. "Cobra," they said. Before I left I had five snakeskins, and one coral necklace bought from a sly old man.

Tourists were not allowed in the street or the plaza before the temple of Jagannath on this day, the day for celebrating the goddess of knowledge. The Saddhu who once fasted sixty days over the cow issue was living here. I was permitted on the roof of the library, from where I could look down to the temple and the plaza. By the temple lay a strapping, healthy, middle-aged man, throwing himself about wildly. His one leg had been amputated at the knee. He must be a holy man, demanding his share of alms. In the United States, this man would have been provided with crutches.

The market stalls were tightly packed with delightful prints in the wild colors of the gods of Jagannath, stylized primitive art, pictures of the temples. The guide selected for me with great zeal. He had the vendor open a new batch of prints. Around us, red saris, green saris, saris of every hue, rings in noses, rings around ankles, filed teeth, broken teeth, no upper teeth at all.

On the piazza, loud noise—rattles and banging of pots. Images of the goddess of knowledge have been brought from the temple, swaying in their chairs as their bearers move through the crowd. The goddesses will be celebrated, and afterward they will become mere clay puppets again, to be thrown into the water, the ocean, or any old waterhole. The wisdom of the teaching of "illusion"—to dissolve.

The driver closed the car door. I was settling back in my seat when I was drawn to look up. I was not sure whether she was made of grayish spider webs, wavering subtly in the scorching heat. Somewhat elevated, as if standing on a stone or even a fence, stood the woman, her eyes fastened on mine. She looked through me, into me, through the plastic and steel body of the car. There was no escape. I felt naked before her to the very depths of my innermost being.

Konarak

In Konarak the fine, feathery ironwood trees and the heavy-rooted banyans surround the temple compound. Boys offer freshly picked coconut. Pilgrims picnic outside the walls. I walk in the shade of trees making a magic circle around the temples. We ascend many disintegrating steps to the three sun-god statues of Vishnu. The guide points to the delicate mesh of the robe, the Nepalese fringes of cultured pearls, and the lion clasp on the belt.

We make detours to the stone horses, their stone enemies under their hooves. We stand before the sun-chariot wheels. We visit (under the sheltering umbrella an Indian holds for me) the medallions of gods and goddesses, of lovers and demons, of single figures of celestial beauty and poise, of two lesbians embracing, of a masturbating beauty, of two men embracing, of lovers surprised by the husband. A complete picture book of copulation, the temple comics of India. There is a hermit, too (only one), tying up his enormous phallus. Demons clasp dancing girls in their arms—females half lion, half woman, with the gleaming face of the great seductress. Mona Lisa in Hindu.

The art on the temple never forgets the lingam; it is given its play in all melodies. The sixty-some positions are acted out in sculptures of such naturalness that I could teach my grandchild without ever uttering an explanatory word. And the last scene I see, which seems like myself, shows old grandma coming home from a pilgrimage to Sarnath or Benares, from the holy River Ganges.

The Pakistani drove me to the airfield for the early flight to

Benares. For the last time.... I was sitting on one of the benches. He was standing. He had been driving for me ten days. I looked up at him, he looked down at me, a strange expression in his face, lips pulling back from his teeth exposed in a snarl. Our eyes met. He, the man, to me, the woman.... He left quickly. I was glad he would not sit in the airplane beside me.

Benares

In Benares I felt at ease. Narrow streets where I bought Kali, the goddess of destruction. I wanted her for the hard core of evil wishes and destructive acts that I carried in my own being. We walked on, peering around the corner at the images behind the golden roofs.

It was too early for the hustle and bustle of pilgrims and Indians on the bathing ghats of the holy River Ganges. We boarded a boat for a pre-sunrise ride. The oarsman first rowed silently upstream. A holy man with stripes across chest and face, a saddhu washing his yellow and red cloth, spreading it on the steps; it would dry shortly. A few women wearing their saris, stood in the river. Steps on the one river bank, bare embankment on the other.

It was before dawn, the hour when the dead rise from the river, taking the morning mist to materialize in soft spider-web shapes over the water. The boat turned, after passing the burning ghats. One corpse shrouded with red designs on the white sheet. The sun rose, a silver, breathing ball through the fog. I opened my hand, slipping a little something into the River Ganges, which would keep it for me. I do believe there is no more trustworthy circumstance in the world than being submerged in its bed.

Kathmandu

The Cambodian guide

A Siva

Kathmandu

On Durbar Square, two sculptured images of Vishnu and his consort look out between the posts of a lovely carved dark-wood window frame on the first floor, watching the crowds go by. People hang their laundry on the steps of the temples to dry. Among garudas, the elephants and lions of the sculptor's grace, infants toddle. The dust of the dry season envelops fannies that short shirts don't quite cover. Eyes dancing with curiosity and the pleasure of living pounce on the passerby, their owner strumming a kind of crude stringed instrument with an open belly, singing a folk song. "Nowadays," the guide says, "they sing mostly about the Nepalese Sherpa who climbed Mount Everest."

On the way to the hotel, we stop at the zoo. Mountain people in heavy, rough, handwoven woolens, with their trotting walk, as if they still carried a burden with the help of a band around the forehead. They are mostly barefoot, clustering around cages that seem too narrow for the animals within. They shoo and clap with boisterous laughter, making the animals snarl in anger or fear.

The golden Buddhas gleam, the oversized scepter lies before the entrance of the temple. Durga looks grim. Vishnu and his consort continue to gaze quietly out on Durbar Square, watching the people go by.

I visit the living goddess, who makes her appearance on a carved wooden balcony in the courtyard of an ancient palace with wood-embroidered entrance. She is a lovely child, made up like a dancer in a festive red dress. I hand money to a little girl who races to the goddess with it. The living goddess comes to the balcony a second time, showing my money between her folded hands. The guide tells me that she is a descendant of a Brahmin or princely family and must abdicate when her first period occurs. She will be free to live, but never to marry, remaining always in the shadow of her childhood-goddess destiny. I imagine that in ancient times the priests would have spared her such a life, mercifully drugging her and sacrificing her in honor of the gods.

We pass a holy man, who arranges his clothes elegantly around himself when he sees us. A temple with closed shrine. When the guide has it opened we see a man sitting in the narrow space before the goddess, who is smeared with henna and decorated with golden chain necklaces. The tiny shrine-dweller turns to us, his face a hateful Durga grimace. He returns to his prayers, bowing before the image, touching his forehead with his knees. The monk closes the shrine.

The giant Buddhist stupa with the huge whitewashed dome is immersed in prayer flags whistling in the wind like the tails of old-fashioned kites. Halfway up, just over the dome, at the base of the tower on all four sides are the painted all-seeing eyes of the Buddha, which look out over the four corners of the earth.

Crossing a bridge, we come upon what I call a Nepalese version of the Versailles mirror room. It is a row of small graceful stone pavilions along one high bank of the narrow river, built close together and each a replica of the others, except for the cupolas, which vary just enough to make the whole more interesting. On the four sides of each pavilion, Roman-arched windows embellished with delicate carving open to the surroundings in all four directions. The most enchanting direction is that looking through the windows from either end of the whole progression along the river bank. From there one sees a chain reaction of procreation: each pavilion harbors a lingam at its center.

Across the water from these pavilions lies the silver gate and golden roof of a Hindu temple that I am not permitted to enter. Monkeys scurry about.

A terrifying figure with swords and other emblems of her destructive power stands in one corner of the Durga Square. It made me shudder in empathy with the Nepalese people who invented this mask of horror. I found among the tiny mountain people ugly, dwarflike figures with Durga faces—frightened masks of primeval horror and anger. I saw, too, the golden Buddha, shaped through the centuries, clear-eyed, with finely chiseled features and royal bearing.

We walk along a small mountain path to a plateau enclosed by hills. A group of amused men stand before a temple, watching a headless rooster fluttering on a stone slab, squirming back and forth. The men holler happily. A little mountain man in dusty clothes grabs the headless creature. Another takes its head out of a boy's hand. The rooster's body is cast down in the center of the slab before an image of crude stone with painted eyes and smeared with blood and henna.

An hour's drive by car (on foot it would take five hours from Durga Square) are pine woods growing thickly and healthy old village houses with wood carving around the window sills and lintels. Steep steps descend to the flowing river. An image within a fenced semicircle built into the cliff. Scarlet spots on the ground near the fence. I stand beside a small boy, pressing my face against the wooden frame of the enclosure. The puddle is blood. A short male stands, a knife in his hands. He puts his foot in the blood smear. A woman bends, taking the red slime in her hands. Men are crowding around the image of Durga, bringing fruit, rice, eggs on green leaves neatly stitched together. Throwing rice at the goddess, they touch her or bow low before her. Goats are brought, ready to be slaughtered. A hen tucked under the arm of one man trustfully allows itself to be washed for the sacrifice. Men wash themselves. A woman washes her feet. "In September," says the guide, "there will be buffaloes, goats, and chickens. We will leave the head for Durga and feast on the rest."

The Peace Corps people from Kathmandu. I had tea with them at the tea house of a gentle Chinese, who refused to take pay for serving us. We were friends. They had lived with rats and dirt under the same conditions as the people from Kathmandu. "My friend," said one of them, slurping his tea in the native manner on returning to civilization, "could not get used to living in a rented room. He was able to sleep again only after he decided to sleep on straw once more and to eat as he had become used to eating with his impoverished friends in Nepal."

Angkor Vat

It was like an ascent of a mountain with many peaks. Starting across the bridge of the moat, source of the eternal liquid-water, and over the vast plain of the territory within the walled courtyard, toward the temple with its grand tower and its four lower corner peaks. Steps lead to galleries with vaulted roofs, crossways through narrow hallways where the sun never enters and the bats fly. One ascent after the other mounting to higher plateaus. On the walls, warriors, gods, and the celestial dancers, the "apsaras" (or divine maidens) in perfect proportion, not too high-breasted, not too hippy, not too elongated or meager—just right for a modern man's idea of a beautiful maiden. I had a photo taken of my guide sitting under an apsara. He touched the frieze, which was polished and shiny from lingering hands like his.

He walked with me through the bat tunnels of Angkor Vat. He climbed high on cornices. "Oh come," he said, "you can do it. Run," he shouted delightedly, starting down a steep, narrow stairway. I ran with him, my hand on his outstretched wrist. I had become his playmate. He wanted to show me his treasures. He raced, with me in the sidecar of his motorized bicycle, through the cremating and burial places for the villagers. He sailed through the village with the highest possible speed, shirt fluttering. He had a flat tire. While he fixed it, I walked across a bridge to look at a primitive but effective waterwheel. Female figures with shawls wrapped over their hats, necks, and shoulders, in long skirts and long-sleeved blouses, looking like wandering mummies. They carried soil for the building of a road, on flat baskets on their heads. A company of soldiers came by all in bathing trunks. They would soak in the river, as most of Angkor Vat seemed to do at this hour of the day.

Some were resting before their stilt houses with bamboo frames and bamboo mats, surrounded by fields and trees— coconut palm, papaya, banana, an applelike fruit, cows on the side of the road, many quiet dogs. I saw a man carrying a dog in his arms like a baby. I saw a very small baby riding on a small

[143]

black pig, held by his father. And of course there was the river flowing lazily, and water buffaloes in moats and ponds.

My guide took me to one of the four entrances of the Bayon, another mountain temple with towers at the cardinal points and one higher central tower. He said he would meet me on the other side. I was to walk through. I was afraid of the forest of smiling, still faces looking down on me.

I ascended steep steps, walked through vaulted, bat-stinking side shrines. At the end of a hallway to my right, a man sat in the lotus position on a cushioned seat on the floor, a dish before him, his hands open. I could see the line of an undershirt around neck and armpit. His dark eyes moved toward me. Drawn by an irresistible urge, I raced toward him with horror. Perpendicular stepping stones stopped my downward rush. I had been like a small fish cascading toward a net. I fled up again, to the uppermost plateau, where I was nearest the still faces, with headgear in the shape of the Naga. Ancestors looking at me with a stillness gained through centuries before I was ever born. I took their presence into my own presence, answering their smiles of timeless stillness with my smile, which was bound in space and time.

I found the way out easily. I ran to the bicycle, directing my guide to the former entrance. I wanted to investigate whether I had actually seen a statue of the Buddha. A man with a broom, who had been moving shiftlessly about in the ruins, accompanied us. He confirmed the fact that there was a Buddha. My guide helped me over the last steep, narrow stone slabs.

"Naga 'Boudha,' " he said. He was highly amused. "She said 'Boudha,' " he repeated.

I stood before my Buddha. He was resting in the lotus posture, on two snake-coil cushions, before him an old tin can with burnt incense sticks. He was of the same clay color all over; he had on no shirt. He could not move his gray clay eyes. I was so glad to know that I had not seen an apparition, even though I had dressed him and made his eyes move, that I turned to the man with the broom and gave him three pieces of paper money. He beamed, receiving it between folded hands, touching it to his forehead. I turned to the Buddha. "Shall I give him something?"

"He will pray for you," the guide answered, still laughing. "He will fly you to heaven with his prayers."

Kalimpong

Along the way to town I saw two of the Tibetan "gilded youths" from the mountains. They walked with great assurance. One had a long, straight black horsehair braid hanging over his white silk cassock. His companion's braid was stuffed under his silk brocade, and he wore a cap with two furry earflaps. They looked me over. I looked them over. Their slanting dark Mongolian eyes were dancing with joyous mischief. As they passed me, they put their hands before their faces, flaps of fur caps whipping with merriment.

I crossed the street to avoid a beggar. Male and bearded, he looked as if he demanded a share of whatever I owned. I resented it. A light shock struck my ankle. I stumbled, but I did not fall. As I walked away I thought, laughing to myself, "You didn't get me."

A young American couple took me to an early Indian movie. Indian gods singing, the lover in the form of Krishna on a throne with horses, elephants, frog, and garuda—Wagner's Lohengrin in India. A heroine throwing her fattened hips about, fluttering eyelids and timid mouth shrinking back in utmost modesty, while rotating her hips and stomach in wild gyrations. The Western woman seems to do just the opposite—eyes, mouth, and hands reaching out seductively, while her innermost sex organs remain on the defensive, even painfully bent backward to avoid touching.

Bangkok, Thailand

"It is time for your happiness," said the boy waiter. He had poured coffee for me, which he had pushed in on a tiered wagon. It did not look like the ominous breakfast contraption waiters usually wheel to your bed in the morning. It looked like a stand for flowers.

Why had nobody told me before I came that Bangkok was cooler, less oppressive, less massive than India? Why had nobody told me before I came that the king of Thailand is still the heart of the country, as a charming lady assistant at the prime minister's travel agency had assured me?

The king was thirty-eight or thirty-nine years old. He had lived in the United States until his twentieth birthday, when he had to choose whether he would live in Thailand or the United States. "And of course," she said, "he chose Thailand." And that is why the guide, a tall, nonchalant young man, can say, "A new freeway," when I point to the elegant curve of steel and concrete, and when I compare an overpass with the foot bridges over Lake Drive in Chicago, he can say proudly, "We had too many pedestrians." Here is a king who seems to take good care of his people. May it always be "time for his happiness."

The Chinese, in sending their China dishes to Thailand hundreds of years ago, broke many during the passage. Someone had the ingenuity to cement the broken pieces over the outer walls of their pagodas, which spiral into the blue Thai sky with crowned peaks and pointed tips soaring. To me, Bangkok's temples were rococo, charming, gay, colorful, irresponsible, reminding me of Walt Disney. The pagoda towers are repeated in the headgear of the dancers. In their heavy gold and silver costumes, they resemble solemnly moving pagodas, with intricate hands fluttering. "It is difficult to learn the mudras," said my guide. "I practiced for two years, but two years are not nearly enough."

These godlike faces bring you coffee in the morning, sell you precious handwoven silks, stand behind you in the sampans, the river boats screened against the sun. Houses are open to the water. Amsterdam and Venice come to mind. The guide remarked about a dam the Americans had helped to build, "You were good to us and we are grateful." It was said easily.

The prime minister's agent had given me an extra tour to see the Emerald Buddha, to see the throne of the king close to the ceiling, to see the reclining Buddha. I walked in the courtyard with its multiple palaces and temples, gold and silver everywhere. The Buddha was still dressed in his winter cloak, his green emerald head peering out from his golden headgear and mesh cloak. The wealth of it all was overwhelming. The guide warned me against stepping on the plank between rooms. It was a protection against ghosts.

One thing was clear. The agent had not confirmed my return ticket. I sat there for two and a half hours waiting for a vacancy, watching him perform. Those godlike features, the full upper lip, the broad under lip, the thin mustache, the nose curving in at the tip—the nose of a cat. Eyes set wide, gleaming brown under heavy eyebrows that were raised toward his temples, dark, sleek hair formed sideburns, ears pointed top and bottom. Not long-eared Buddha lobes, but small elegant ears, set high. From the front, his face was heart-shaped, wide at the eyes, the chin firm but not aggressive, with a perfect cleft.

He glided in and out of the room, each step vibrating to the hip, the whole body limp with waiting. He gave me a quick smile through slanted eyes and half-opened mouth. The heavens opened when the Buddha smiled. He danced between his desk and the ticket counter. When he came at last, nonchalantly striding on cat paws to give me my ticket, he had not a care in the world. He strutted away, his dark glasses fastened at his agile hip. I saw the back of his head. My cat had no brains—a straight line up from his firm, proud neck—no room for brains.

The Caribbean Islands, 1967

HANNAH ALONE

Antigua

The island people are gentle. They are friendly—not *for* us but *with* us. Gradually they will replace their white compatriots. At the moment, little of yesterday remains and little of tomorrow is to be seen. The present means no more than listening to the lapping of waves against the coral shore. The monotonous beat of the tide, soon picked up by the beat of native drums, is accompanied by the feminine whisper of palm leaves along the lagoon.

The old buildings along the harbor, dating from the days of British colonial rule, were not pompous but dignified. The admiral's house, with its thin, stick-like balcony railings, reminded me of Philip C. Johnson's New York State Theater at Lincoln Center. In this building, with its whitewashed walls and slender balcony, the admiral and his British adjuncts, splendidly attired, represented the British Empire with arrogance and dignity.

The design of the outdoor hotel bar reminded me of Philip Johnson's Roofless Church in New Harmony. It has a four-sided, triangular, wooden roof dipping almost to the ground, lower in fact than the shingled, beehive-shaped canopy at the front of the Roofless Church.

The lovely basketweave of the wood-framed chairs was of Spanish origin. The brown glazed earthenware cooking pots were native. Piled atop one another, they served as columns for the railings separating the outside dining space from the bench.

[149]

Standing alone, they became ashtrays. The pattern for the curtains in my cottage looked as though it was lifted from some French palace.

The drive from the airfield was abominably depressing. There were the usual houses on stilts with their weathered wooden shingles. And for the poorer natives, there were one-room shacks with straw-thatched, or sometimes corrugated iron, roofs (which must become intolerably hot). Before many of the huts, raw sewage flowed in open ditches. There were hydrants spaced at intervals along the road for those without running water, and virtually all of the native huts were without it. There was no electricity except in the hotels. We came to an open lagoon surrounded by young palms, a road through a grayish-green lawn—the hotel. The food turned out to be not particularly good. No papayas, no mangoes.

"People don't grow things any more," said my driver. He gave me a laborious but thorough lecture on the obligations of Antiguan citizenship now that the British were gone. "Now *everyone* has to take care of the island." He reminded me of a donkey I had seen standing and braying on the hard greased spot before a native hut. Not a melodious sound, but so expressive. The beast drags a load, carries a burden, or a man, or perhaps two children. But the amount it will bear always falls below expectations.

"This all used to be cotton," he said, pointing to the right of the road. "Our people are lazy, and they don't want to wear work clothes any more." He pointed to the left. "This was a sugarcane field, but now people are lazy, they go to work for the hotels." We drove past a very modest group of American-style houses standing on the dusty soil without gardens, trees, or any attempt at landscaping. "A black man bought all this land. He builds houses and rents them to Americans." The driver then pointed ahead. "The government took this land for cattle grazing." A pause. "We used to grow yams here. Now we import them and they're very expensive, about twelve cents a pound."

Tourists are the major commodity. The woman who cleaned my room gave me a neat speech. "Please come back or we will have no work!"

[150]

Bequia

Bequia

Gladys had asked, "Do you like Tom?"

I answered, "Power can be neither liked nor disliked."

I knew of few people like him. Piling rock upon rock, he built Moonhole, his nest amid the powers of nature. Walls high as cliffs, steps irregular as nature; just enough artifice to make it safe for humans.... Whittling aimlessly at a piece of root and being pleasantly surprised at the result.... Dogs huddled at his feet. He often treated them better than people.... Always creating but never planning. He built in curves, adding stones to walls,

[151]

taking pleasure in crooked spaces. There were never many right angles in the houses he built.

He had so many voices: the voice of the host, trying to be there even when he was not; the voice of the master, giving orders, guiding, directing; the voice of the wanderer of his island, observing and showing others; the voice of his women friends, coaxing, explaining, understanding; and the voice of a mischievous, willful, utterly free spirit of nature.

Very often he had no face at all. I could not have drawn it as I could the beautiful medallion face of his wife.

I loved his empty, brooding face. I did not love his old-womanish face, hostile to everyone and everything, refusing to accept any law. No planning. Planning was a threat.

Besides this amorphous power, Gladys's compassionate face emerged with clarity. She was responsible for maintaining an orderly routine, teaching and training the boys and girls who had their own share of unreality, floating on the steps like windblown flowers or joyously climbing mountains like young goats. It was difficult to teach them responsibility. They became sullen if not coaxed carefully along.

I heard the echo of her voice in those of the boys and girls who served me, patiently explaining what it was they had brought in for breakfast, lunch, or dinner.

I heard her voice reprimanding a boy who had dropped a telegram in the ocean, "I am very mad at you," but it conveyed no real anger.

•

Gladys wouldn't look at me as I told her my story. She said "This sort of thing never happens to Tom and me." Did she mean to imply I had been the cause of the native's hostility?

The blacks had been sitting on the boardwalk that runs along the harbor for several hours before my white friend and I arrived. My friend was walking ahead of me, delighted to be in a completely black environment for the first time in his life, when I noticed a sign reading "Black is Beautiful," framed by two mock-wooden rifles. Three men were sitting under it on the concrete boardwalk. One, a man with a shaven head, paler than his two companions, was sitting in the lotus posture. The second was crouched on his knees. I did not pay attention to the third, but he was dark. The set-up seemed military.

My friend was now far ahead and I was the only white in the street. Refugees who had fled the other side of the island where a volcano was threatening to erupt were streaming by. Tomorrow would be carnival day.

Two years before I had walked behind a carnival procession of people dressed in fancy costumes that resembled American Indian outfits: crowns of feathers, spears, drums, trumpets, and streamers of all colors. A woman standing on the sidewalk suddenly spat at me. She missed, but the experience was still disconcerting. I kept walking with the procession, but the joy of it was gone for me. I turned to go back to my hotel and two of the dancers followed, asking me to join them. I did so, and they did an extra noisy and cheerful dance for me. I clapped my hands to the beat, and, when it was over, I thanked them and left.

That same year, Sydney had told me, "Twenty years from now the white landowners will be gone. There will be bloodshed and they will be dispossessed." He had sounded sorrowful. Sydney was the owner of a small fleet of cars on the island. He knew every traveler and may have had some white blood himself. It was often difficult to cope with his half-native, half-educated ideas, but I liked and respected him.

Now Sydney was dead and I stood alone on the wide street before a sign saying "Black is Beautiful," and a grim, shaven, light-skinned native sitting in the lotus posture. I should not have looked down at him. Sydney would have advised me not to. "Don't stop whenever you see any kind of gathering or demonstration." He would have known the mood of the people and insisted I go in his car or he would at least have walked beside me.

The light-skinned man made a harsh gesture, raising his hand. "Go away!" he said in an ugly voice. I looked down at him. At that moment I felt too happy to be disturbed.

"Why do you want me to go away?" I asked. I liked him. I liked everything around me. Why should anyone tell me to leave?

"Go away!" he repeated.

[153]

"Why should I?"

"Because you are white."

That made little sense to me. I did not think white. I was a human being enjoying myself. Why shouldn't I also be allowed to feel "Black is Beautiful"?

As the sun became brighter their glistening skins darkened in the sharp shadows on the enclosed boardwalk.

"You know," I said, "when we are skeletons we all become white. No color distinction then." The shaven man's face twisted in astonishment, and one of his companions emitted a loud breathing sound. It might have become a laugh. We might have laughed together, embraced, and parted.

But the light-skinned man said again, "Go away!" His voice was hoarse, as though something were choking him.

"I'm sorry," I said. My friend waved at me from down the street and I walked to meet him. Behind me was a stony silence.

But there were other occasions when black and white had enjoyed themselves without any qualms. There had been a stunning young Negro on the mailboat to Bequia. On his lap a black girl wiggled joyously under the hand he had inserted at just the right place. I, the white woman sitting opposite him, did not create any feeling of disturbance. Sheer enjoyment on both sides.

And then there was the stormy return trip on a sailboat that could hold only sixteen people, when I sat with an arrogant-looking, well-dressed young black couple. The captain had put on his raincoat and watery mountains surged against the boat, throwing me violently about. I was not seasick but utterly exhausted. The ship fell back suddenly and I slipped from my seat to the bottom of the boat, trying desperately to grasp hold of something. The black girl bent down and I took her hand while her husband reached out for me. I groaned, "Please, let me hold on to you. It's all that can help me now." Comfortingly they held on to my hands for at least three quarters of an hour while I shook between the waves.

After we arrived he told me he was a New York band leader. There had been no black or white skin between us. We had been made of glass, translucent to our white bones. They had been like daughter and son bent comfortingly over their mother to console her with their strong compassionate hands.

[154]

There had been other incidents I had only heard about. Somebody had ransacked Tom and Gladys's house while they were dining in the gallery with their guests. The thief had known exactly where to find the guests' money and jewels, but nobody implicated the servants. When the theft was discovered, the native community had taken over and recovered the stolen jewels and money. They had neither wanted nor needed the police.

But had a delicate chain uniting black and white been broken? Had a mutual trust been violated? Or had something perhaps been gained by the black community's initiative in recovering the stolen money?

San Juan

Houses with wrought-iron balconies and carved wood railings. . . . Wide, tree-filled plazas, blue cobblestone streets, native music, an outdoor television. . . . A gate in the old fortified wall leads to a road along the harbor. A battleship is steaming powerfully in to shore. On a plateau between the fortifications and the harbor lies the old Spanish cemetery, resplendent with shiny marble angels and statues of Christ on the Cross in profile against the open sea. Girls with roses held in their laps and wings on their shoulders; marble folds clinging around chaste, maidenly breasts and thighs. . . .

There is a decaying circular chapel and nearby, bordering on the cemetery, is an open, arched hallway honeycombed with cells for hundreds of coffins. It works like a bread oven. Slabs of rock are lifted away from the entrance to let the coffin slide in. The slab is then refastened, the body decomposes and, in time, another will follow.

Between the fortified wall and the ocean is another plateau, this one covered with shacks built so close together they are literally on top of one another. I walk in the roadway alongside the first rows of huts. Street kids are spinning tops in the wide irregular lane. I ask a woman standing alone in front of her shack for directions. She obliges but eyes me suspiciously. I pass a fierce-looking beggar. The boys spinning their tops glance up as I approach. Stopping, I say, "Spin them! My grandson loves to do it all the time." They spin, and I move from boy group to boy group making them spin their tops until I come to a steep iron stairway leading back to the main street. Some men walk toward me staring fixedly and without a smile. After they pass I look back and am relieved to see an American soldier. It has become dark. Later I am told that that afternoon a group of people in the neighborhood had attempted to defy the establishment of a new police station. Three police officers had been killed.

The next afternoon I try to go swimming but there is such an assembly of raw meat lying on a small beach of the new, high-rise hotel that I choose instead to have luncheon in the expensive, air-conditioned dining room inside, having my cocktail, smoking a cigarette, eating "a little something" and enjoying the sweet anonymity of a big hotel.

Mexico, 1968

HANNAH ALONE

Mexico City

Light from the bulbs in the five-layered crystal chandelier, a thousand times reflected in bangles of prisms, dances with rainbow colors, seducing passersby on their way to the Zocalo. Entering the heavy, modern glass door and for the first time ascending the twelve steps to the oval lobby, one stops to admire the pair of oversized, gold-latticed, empty bird cages that frame the entrance and its malachite and golden door handles. Suddenly the cages reveal themselves as elevators gliding lustily up and down between three flourishing balconies, swinging past stucco pillars with gilded Corinthian capitals. The pattern of the stained-glass elevator panels is repeated in the oval ceiling, mounted in flowery designs, shining in green, lilac, and blue. The lobby, with its gentle green carpeting, seems like an old-fashioned garden. Globules of light grow between the circular rosebuded sofas and their delicate golden tables, flanked by low, red-velvet stools. Here, everything is light and gay. None of the heavy plushness of my hotel in Chicago, the blood-red lobby of which recalls the entrance to a slaughterhouse. A Frenchman had bought the Zocalo as a department store and had it converted into a hotel.

Perhaps there was some Mexican-Indian influence in all the joyousness. I had seen the same colors and design in Oaxaca's cathedral.

Page boys in short, brocaded green jackets and waiters in red jackets stalk their clientele through the lobby. It is indeed a happy hunting ground.

On the Balcony

I

Just before sunrise I observe a being of indeterminate sex clad in a shocking-pink sweater and nondescript pants, its face obscured by a broad-brimmed hat, digging around in the hotel garbage pails. The creature removes the lid from one of the trash barrels, places it on the next container and begins sifting through the contents. It selects what looks to be pieces of discarded meat, bread, and fruit. Replacing the lid, the being departs with the shreds of yesterday's dinner from the tables of the rich.

II

In the evening, I watch as two young policemen harass an attractive woman selling ice cream on the street. A gigantic dark-skinned Mexican appears from the other side of the street and approaches the three. The two policemen abruptly let the girl go and vanish in the direction of the Zocalo. The giant speaks to the woman, who answers with open-armed gratitude. At the same time she makes defiant gestures in the direction in which the police had disappeared. The protector of the poor leaves the scene. People who had moved away during the woman's encounter with the Law again crowd around her to buy ice cream.

Around the Zocalo

Beggars tread the pavement under the Zocalo's colonnade. Most are blind or crippled, but there are also healthy ones who lean against the walls between the display windows and hold up toys to the passing crowd. They sell toys that will break if you touch them, watches that won't tick if you wind them; all the shabby leftovers of mechanized civilization.

Farther down the street are wide-windowed shops displaying the arts and crafts of the Mexican people. They offer delightful figurines in many different materials—wood, metal, and leather—celebrating living, loving, and dying in sad or humorous designs.

[158]

The Cathedral

I

The interior of the Cathedral had been neglected. The organ had burnt out and not been replaced or repaired; the stone floor seemed unwashed. The side altars looked shabby behind dusty wooden lattices. The church had the atmosphere of an abandoned barn. The only open side chapel contained a black Christ on the Cross with a heavy red sash tied about his black wooden thighs. People were kneeling, praying, and buying candles that they light to the suffering God. A skeletal, gray man, stick in hand, bustled around the candles, harassing a dignified, middle-aged man who had—or so it seemed to the old skeleton with the stick—displaced the old man's candle from its position directly beneath the Saviour's image. The old man tore out the other's candle and moved it far to the right where the Redeemer would be unable to see it even if he could raise his tear-stained face. The reprimanded worshiper remained praying and the old skeleton hobbled away.

II

Mass was performed in the side chapel. Priests clad in red- and gold-threaded brocade moved before the altar. The sharp tingle of the bell celebrating the transubstantiation filled me with the same sweet terror as the human bone trumpets had in Nepal. Incense, from the golden lamps swinging in the hands of one brocaded priest, covered the altar in an obscuring mist. An intense fragrance from the burning incense filled the chapel. Four slim youths stood earnestly at the bench in front of me. I had seen them earlier kidding around outside, but now the magic of the priest's intoning voice had gripped them. The mystic inner music had reached their ears and they would kneel now without shame, unprotected by sheltering curtains, between the feet of the priest who had heard them in the confessional.

III

It was dusk when I stepped out of the Cathedral. Tiny lights, strung along the outline of the major monuments and churches, had been switched on, making the stone seem luminous. Under

[159]

Virgin of Soledad in Oaxaca, Mexico

Head in the private collection of H. Leigh, Oaxaca

the arcade, amid the surging evening crowd, a husky, older Mexican was horsing around with a handsome youth. The man took hold of the boy around the neck, another boy grabbed the legs of the first, and the two turned him upside down. It was all done silently and without a trace of expression. The husky man began lowering the tortured adolescent's head toward the curb. I looked away, hoping to find a policeman who could intervene, but when I turned again to the trio the man had placed the youth back on his feet. The three walked silently off together through the gradually dispersing crowd.

The Beggar

Returning from luncheon at the Ritz, in a narrow street leading to the Zocalo, I was accosted by a haggard young woman wrapped in a gray shawl. There had been beggars all along the way, but this one left her sitting position on the sidewalk and refused to let me escape. Small children clung to her torn skirts. She stretched out her left hand to me, a picture of misery and starvation. In an upsurge of deep pity, I tore out my coin purse and poured the considerable change into her dirty hands, which closed quickly over the booty. Embarrassed by my public display of emotion, I hurried on. A woman walking alongside me turned toward me, "Don't feel too sorry for them," she said pleasantly. "That was one of the Marias, as we call them here in the city. They come in from the farm belt for better wages and working conditions. The government provides them with housing, the Mafia takes away their good clothes, dresses them in rags, and even furnishes them with small children should they have none of their own. All to make them look more pitiful. As you see, it works. That wretch won't even keep the money you gave her. It all goes to the pimp." She walked on while I stood and blushed, feeling humiliated and defeated.

Palace de Bellas Artes

More than twenty years ago I had seen the Folklore ballet danced with passionate simplicity on a tiny wooden stage, in a dark, overcrowded room. This time, at the Palace de Bellas Artes, I had first to face the famous Tiffany curtain, which reminded me of my hotel ceiling. The performance was far removed from what I considered "art." Luxurious stage sets replaced imagination. The ballet had become mechanistic perfection. Slick fluency, Hollywood costumes, and clicking heels and toes.

The most astonishing feat in the program was the deer dance. The dancer's identification with the spirit of the animal was so intense I still insist I saw an actual deer. The antler head, tossed gracefully in startled fright, was not a mask covering a human face. The human had disappeared. What remained was pure animal nature.

Comanjilla

Located a thousand feet above sea level, the Hacienda was bordered by a semicircle of brown-grassed hills. The old farmhouse, with its ten rooms that give out onto a patio lined by a heavy, arched colonnade, was still intact. Humboldt was supposed to have slept there, but the house had since been enlarged. There was a spacious garden with palms, shrubs, and flowers surrounding the main house, motel units, and swimming pool.

Every morning the hotel guests would start down the gentle sloping road. It was not too difficult to limp back up for luncheon, even if one's arthritis was in the legs. In the cactus groves to the right of the road lay the Indians' waterholes. Cacti piled high as totem poles—tree cacti and still another variety with yellow flowers stood surrounding black-barked perul trees.

Narrow paths led to the hot-water brook where the Indian women did the family wash, and afterward soaped themselves (sometimes nude) and their children (always nude), while the laundry, spread out on cactus and tree branches, dried in the hot sun. Up some steep steps from the brook was an open-air toilet for the laundry washers. I had seen something similar in Pátzcuaro when a whole tribe jumped down from their trucks, slipped down their pants and began fertilizing the fields in unison. Here, human waste lay stinking as it dried among fragments of splintered, green Coca-Cola bottles. Somewhat farther down, between gnarled branches and firm, olive-colored perul leaves, were visible the black-haired heads and brown shoulders of the washing males. The water flowed and cleansed while transistor radios blared.

At first, I found the outdoor grooming very romantic. The Indians were keeping to their old ways, perhaps performing time-honored rituals. After I visited the Indian village, which the proprietors of the Hacienda had so generously built for their employees (the entire village was in the service of the hotel), it no longer seemed so romantic. The Indian dwellings were small, shabby, and without any plumbing. The hot-water spring under the perul trees and cactus hedges was their only bathroom, their W.C. the path alongside.

"Our" hot springs boiled behind the old farmhouse amid sulphur-yellow and white-streaked brown soil. It was a minature Yellowstone without Old Faithful and surrounded by palm trees and many colored beehives. The gardener boiled his luncheon eggs in a tiny, always bubbling spring.

One of the deeper-lying springs was hooked up to a sauna. A plastic chute was used to bring the steam up into a little plastic tent with a wooden bench inside. One could sit there, entirely wrapped in the precious steam, inhaling the sulphur-tinged vapors, for as long as one could stand it.

The "frog pond," one among the many heaving holes, overshadowed by trees, overgrown by duckweed, overflown by dragonflies and hopping with fish and frogs, contained "pure" drinking water. We at the hotel did not drink it. Our water came in bottles and I brushed my teeth with soda. The Indians, or so I heard, got their drinking water from a spring high in the mountains. The Hacienda's proprietor took great pains to persuade them to help themselves from the "frog pond." But the Indians refused. They were used to carrying their water down the mountain on donkeys in large earthen jugs, along paths the goats had made where, perhaps in the lower areas, cattle grazed on the coarse grass interspersed between cactus candelabra and the black trunks of the olive-like perul trees.

Around noon, when the sun stood high, the swimming pool would come alive with old people. Senior citizens with protruding stomachs, flabby thighs, and red, blotched faces hung on to the railing of the hotel pool. Immersed in the warm fluid, sporting all manner of headgear as protection against the glaring sun, they pressed their feet against the pool walls for exercise. Some of the more audacious would even venture to swim back and forth across the pool. They chattered over each other's heads, greedy for contact. This was the communion of the old and sick. Three-legged after the bath, they shuffled along the cool concrete hallways to their rooms, chattering comfortably about their ailments. Sickness had become the norm. Sickness acquired, sickness fought, old age's misfortunes endured: such were the themes of their communal monologues. Gray skin cannot be livened by night creams, nor can hands that have become brown-spotted lizard claws. Rings on arthritic fingers do not divert, swollen ankles and flabby breasts are not things of beauty. But worst is the mental decay.

An old man sitting on the porch watched benevolently as bell-boys hurried by with the luggage of new arrivals. "How nice it is," he said, "to see someone able to carry so many heavy bags all at once."

The 1936 Travel Diary of Paulus

The following brief excerpts are taken from Paulus's extensive day-to-day account of his first return to Europe after he and his family escaped from Hitler. When this diary was published in its entirety by Harper & Row, Jerald C. Brauer wrote in the introduction to the book: "The most remarkable thing about the diary is the flood of people that pour over the pages. It seems impossible that one man could have known so many people—an astounding variety of people—professors, artists, musicians, politicians, students, businessmen, the great and the humble. He knew them and was concerned about them. To know a person does not mean to be acquainted with him. To know a person is to encounter him as someone with hopes, fears, convictions, dreams, pettiness, and generosity. Tillich's knowledge of people, of his friends, was of this quality. The diary reflects this with great clarity." The trip lasted from April to September of 1936.

Holland

[Family and friends come from within Germany to visit Paulus.]
M. L. tells us, and proves by her own example, how well informed people are in Germany. She describes a kind of arithmetic book in which the schoolchildren get this type of problem: "One bomb kills twenty people; how many people can twenty bombs kill?" She says it is no longer possible to take an ironically superior attitude; one must reject the whole thing

matter-of-factly, though carefully. Everyone is quite aware of the election swindle.

•

I get up tired. There is a moist wind from the south. Work. A violent discussion with Trudchen on National Socialism.

Earlier, at lunch, we had an explosion over the Jewish question and the boycott. I identify myself with the fate of the Jews. In the evening I read my program outline aloud. Discussion, especially over the section on foreign policy. That night I have a ghastly dream: my eyes are going to be put out. Next morning M. L. analyzes my dream as stemming from a sense of aggression from the family.

•

I have talked with Frede and Trude day after day. Trudchen is desultory and a convinced National Socialist; Frede more critical but full of hatred against foreigners and refugees, especially Jews. Conversation is very difficult because of the way Trudchen jumps from one subject to another. I can talk about a number of issues with Frede, but not with Trudchen. Elisabeth is infinitely more objective and easier to get along with. Erhardt is very quiet. All behave in a somewhat pedagogical way toward me. M. L. is silent.

•

At six, I meet Frau v. Bock who begs me to look after Elisabeth. She tells me that her father [a general dismissed by Hitler] has not yet been reinstituted. And that Erhardt, unfortunately, has become very careful—like Elisabeth. She tells me that the secretaries at the German legation are treated badly; that Ribbentrop caused Hoetsch to have a heart attack. She talks of suitcases standing packed and ready after the Germans had marched into the Rhineland; about a report from the Bureau of Statistics that only 53 percent voted for Hitler. She says that none of the people she personally knows voted for him. To listen to her, nobody at all is for him.

•

I am going to Eushede at the German border to meet Staehlin. Lilly takes the same train all the way to Berlin. Communism and the things that happened to her have turned her into a mature human being. She tells me that for a year and a

[*168*]

half Fritz was facing the threat of imprisonment every day. They used to say good-by every morning as if it were forever.

During my lectures Lilly made friends with the Communist couple. The man was so deeply stirred after my final lecture that he came the next day, all the way from Amsterdam, and asked me to turn my ideas into a pamphlet for clandestine distribution. I am writing this in a little waiting-room restaurant, waiting for Staehlin to arrive.

Finally he arrives, and we talk for four hours. It is one of my most important encounters on this entire journey. We start immediately, with the problem closest to his heart: the Confessing Church. His report is shattering: the most rigid, fanatical orthodoxy; anyone who disagrees on questions of dogma is instantly expelled. Denunciations are the order of the day. Everyone is required to submit unconditionally to the brotherhood counsels. A few weeks ago fourteen students boycotted his seminar because he was conducting exams together with "German Christians." Anyone who dares disagree is accused of heresy. On the other hand, the church committees are slowly but steadily working toward some kind of cooperation, for instance in Saxony. However, they may fail in the attempt, and if they do, there will be nothing left but the orthodox sect, fruit of Barthian theology.

Staehlin judges the world situation of Protestantism exactly as I do, which is to say negatively. He sees it defenseless against Catholicism. At this point I read him the last paragraph of my "Protestantism in the Present World Situation," and he takes it down in shorthand. Amazing how much we still think alike after four years of separation! The idea of the religious order lies at the center of his thinking. He expresses his own conviction: that all really decisive matters cannot really take effect for at least fifty years. He feels we must arm ourselves against the time of chaos. He himself has asked to be retired; he wants to become the abbot of a Protestant monastery he founded near Rothenburg, Fulda. If the Kultusministerium refuses to pension him, he plans simply to quit. When he told this to his dean, the dean said, after a moment of shocked silence: "You still have a future. What you propose here is senseless."

Staehlin says that work at the universities is hopeless, work at

[169]

the theological faculties senseless. Men from secular life—not young theology students—should be the leaders of the communities. He rejects Nazism unconditionally. He thinks that those who have gone through it might develop a new pagan Christianity which might be able to overcome the confessional split. He tells me that the leading Catholic liturgist, a Benedictine monk, said to him that they and his (Staehlin's) wing of the Protestant Church would someday fight side by side against Rome. But on the whole he is very pessimistic about the possibility of realizing his ideas in Germany. What he would like best would be to establish a German branch of the Anglican Church.

Staehlin talks of demonic sacraments and analyzes the Nazi swastika as a cross with claws instead of tails such as the real Indian sun wheel has. He is reading Goethe's *Chromatology* in order to analyze the color *brown* (the color of the Nazis). He says he rarely has visions but is now plagued by one that shows Germany turned into a battlefield. On the day of Potsdam he cried all afternoon.

I broach the social angle. He admits that this is his weak point, but insists that the brotherhood's apolitical attitude and community organization must be regarded as symbolic. He does admit that such an attitude may bring with it the danger of seeming to support those in power. There is a contradiction here concerning their basic intentions.

The total impression of our meeting: the idea of the religious order is encountered everywhere. Nobody believes any longer that the masses can be directly reeducated. This is a retreat, to be sure. But it also makes it possible for the leading intellectual and religious forces to regroup and gather strength.

At eight o'clock we say good-by, our friendship reaffirmed.

Paris

We go to one of the big cafés on the Champs Elysées. Mrs. Kleyer tells me about an evening with Picasso and others, all, she assures me, enthusiastic followers of the Front Populaire. All

[170]

leftist France is in a fever of expectation, whereas the rightists are frightened and are taking their money out of the country. The strike was a little revolution. The employees had barricaded themselves inside the buildings, behind lowered shutters, and it never even occurred to the government to send in the police. At night the men slept in the buildings and the women brought food to them. Blum is greatly respected, but there are doubts about his leadership qualities.

•

She suffers a great deal, does not look well, and feels unhappy in Paris, like most of the others. She tells heartrending stories about refugees in Paris: judges selling books from door to door; lawyers delivering milk and vegetables; a rash of suicides.

Switzerland

At 11:30, at Karl Barth's. Extremely animated friend-to-friend conversation in which we trade insults. I tell him about Barth in America whereupon he declares that under the circumstances he won't have to go there. I say that, unlike him, I feel closer to the early Christians than to the Reformation; that, for me, the criterion is all-important; that I feel his letter contradicted his theology. To which he can only add that he could not have done otherwise three years ago. He feels my existence in America is providential. We part as great friends.

•

I meet Ministerialdirektor Richter. He gives me his view of the situation; it sounds even more hopeless than mine. He says that things of unimaginably low morality are continuously happening. He feels the universities are dead, transformed into mere cadet training grounds. He thinks that war is inevitable. He was at the Baumgartens', too, last night, taking part in the discussion. He does not believe in a militarist-monarchist solution. He himself is studying theology in Basel, lives near the border because of his pension, has to cross the border twice a day.

[*171*]

London

Dada Langer talks about her own escape from Germany by way of a cemetery near Saarbrücken. As soon as she had crossed the border into France, she went to the first French governor she could find. He tested her—to see if she really was a student—by asking: "Where is Professor Tillich?" Answer: "In New York." Correct. ". . . Professor Wertheimer?" "On his way to New York." Correct. This was all the proof he asked.

•

Mrs. Schairer is in slacks and blouse, looks fresh, but has aged. They have a charming house with garden. After lunch we take coffee outside on the lawn. Schairer has completely broken with the Nazis, but he openly and wistfully longs to be in Germany. His wife is strongly anti-Nazi, paints a horrifying picture of Germany. The youth problem: fifteen million young people working for rearmament in Europe. Radicalization and disappointment of German youth. Institute for Youth Studies. The tragic self-destruction of the older generation—taking one wrong step after another. Their talk with Schacht, who is completely subservient to Hitler. I talk with Mrs. Shairer about Elsa—Elsa Bradnstrom.

Paris

To Mme. Rappaport, now Perade. The Riezlers had given her my address. She has not been able to get her money out of Germany, and is now working hard for some fashion magazines. She is pretty as always (no longer paints her fingernails red). Recently she was the last person to be fired from a German magazine. Her editor-in-chief was not allowed to have any further contact with her. She wants to come to America, for her own sake and especially for the sake of Beckmann, who has been utterly crushed in Germany.

Holland

A young writer comes and brings a book. He stays for lunch, and afterward he and I have a long talk about the psychology of Holland's young people. His views are similar to Schairer's: disintegration, visions of war and death. As an example, he describes a recent art exhibit which showed a marked emphasis on death.

Switzerland

To Meng's, who invites me for dinner. Excellent conversation about psychoanalysis and religion, especially the problem of whether the power to fulfill his own meaning is inherent in man. He postulates that every human being brings a "program" into the world, whose fulfillment is, at the same time, the fulfillment of the meaning of his life. We call for his wife at the theater, walking through ancient streets. She has white hair but seems young. We cross the Rhine and walk past nightspots full of soldiers and students who sing and drink wine: Europe!

I go back to Schmidt's and we talk until two in the morning, over a bottle of good Swiss wine. I am astonished to discover that Schmidt has reverted to a primitive orthodoxy of inspiration. He considers the virgin birth a photographically demonstrable fact; the same with the rest of the miracles, because the Bible says so— such as the empty tomb and others. I can only think: my predictions have come true even faster than I expected.

After a visit to Conrad Ferdinand Meyer's grave, I take a streetcar to the Odéon to meet Hirschfeld. We eat in a nice old place where the sound of the Sunday evening bells is so overpowering that one can hardly talk. Later we discuss various books published by Oprecht on which he (Hirschfeld) has worked. At the moment the most important—though not the best—is *I Cannot Keep Silent*. His work on Langhof's *Moor-*

soldaten consisted in taking out the most gruesome parts and placing the beautiful passage about the prisoners' theater in the center of the book. He was also instrumental in getting Langhof across the border. He himself was in Russia for a long time, studying the Russian theater. This brought him into close contact with the Russians; Eisenstein wanted to keep him there. But he preferred to stay in his embattled position in Zurich. He seems to have many underground connections. We walk back and forth on the Limmat Bridge, with the moon and thousands of lights across the lake. Later we sit in a beer garden where a band plays a medley of German songs. At ten o'clock we go to Medicus's. Sitting beside an open window wall, we drink two bottles of wonderful wine. Medicus and Hirschfeld have a lively conversation about—I think—the world situation. But the moment is much too beautiful to be reminded about it.

•

I get up at six, after a deathlike sleep. Breakfast in the garden; intoxicating fragrance of linden blossoms.

Then I leave for Zurich. The clouds are streaming with rain. To Oprecht, where I return the books. I try to locate Wendriner, finally send him a telegram; then I have a long talk with Oprecht. Serious worries over Spain. Every time I want to go to Spain, another Fascist revolution breaks out and prevents me. If the Fascists should win, the effect on France would be incalculable. Oprecht also feels that Central Europe should be ceded to Hitler; nothing is being done in Danzig; Austria is being conquered by means of quiet infiltration. Even now, anti-German books are slowly disappearing from Austrian bookstores. The German part of Switzerland and German Czechoslovakia are unprotected. Swiss newspapers are pervaded by a general sense of existential anxiety.

Lunch with Bernese wine at the Hotel Simplon. At the Café Odéon I meet Hirschfeld, Wendriner, and Salome Boller. Wendriner and I take a walk along the lake. He is terribly depressed; a doctor told him a few days ago that he has a heart defect. He must live in Switzerland, at an altitude of 300 feet. He is unhappy because all the older German literature is being sold off for a few pennies; he was with Thomas Mann, who, he says, is very happy and has completely freed his inner self from Germany.

•

Stepun in the department of economics, with four students and many unmatriculated listeners: the best is the historian Kuehn, who speaks very openly against the regime. Stepun has social contact with Nazis and enjoys pulling the Gestapo's leg. He feels that the Nazis are the framework within which it is still possible to work, refuses to attack the regime as such. I report on the European situation and on Hitler's victory on the Continent. He is deeply shaken, feels that he has taken Nazism too lightly.

England

Around 6:30 we arrive at Blickling Hall, one of the most famous country seats of British nobility. Dutch Renaissance, dating back to 1620. I am immediately taken in hand by the butler and two manservants. One of them takes my suitcase in order to unpack it. For this purpose I must leave the room, so that he can have a free hand. Later I will find all my things beautifully arranged and distributed.

Downstairs, Oldham shows me two marvelous paintings by Holbein, a Van Dyck, a Canaletto, etc. On the staircase stands a wooden statute of Anne Boleyn, who was born in a house nearby. There is also a huge wall tapestry, a gift from Catherine II to one of Lord Lothian's ancestors who was ambassador to St. Petersburg. There are several portraits by Lawrence and many other ancestral portraits all bearing an unmistakable family resemblance to the present lord, the last, childless, heir of the house of Lothian. I meet Lord Lothian himself before dinner—he is in evening clothes, of course—a powerful man who would look very well wearing armor. He is a member of the House of Lords and he knows everyone.

During an hour-long walk, Lord Lothian explains his own theory to me: the Western democracies are to protect themselves by keeping aloof from the quarrels of European dictators.

Germany is to be appeased and allowed to gain supremacy over Central Europe. France and Belgium will thus be safeguarded.

In the evening the Foreign Office representative tells me that he considers Lothian's theory untenable. He feels that Germany must never be allowed to gain that much power. He adds that England is always politically paralyzed when faced with real fanaticism because the English imagination cannot grasp a situation that allows of no compromise.

In the debates over the upcoming Oxford conference there are two distinctly different viewpoints: the Lutheran-German and the Anglo-Saxon. I feel that I have somehow come to stand on the boundary between the two.

After the debate I walk through the park alone. I hear, for the first time in two and a half years, that unforgettable concert of bird song. I meet Lord Lothian, who is also walking alone. As he puts it: he is seeking respite in nature from human problems. He shows me some pheasants and dozens of deer. None of these animals is ever hunted.

After dinner we have some informal conversation. Then early to bed. The Lothian library, which was bought from a French cardinal, is housed in a long, narrow hall. A Clouet hangs in the study.

·

Next, a visit to the slums which date back to the beginning of the nineteenth century. Aesthetically interesting streets composed of one-story houses which contain small flats with comparatively good furniture. Every street. Women in shawls; completely emaciated bodies. There is a sense of hopelessness, caused by unemployment which, in turn, is due to England's loss of the Indian cotton market. The younger people are being relocated in southern industrial areas. The remaining population gives a resigned impression—unaggressive. At the same time there is some sort of festivity going on—a government anniversary is being celebrated.

I spend some time preparing my lecture. At seven o'clock, dinner with Canon Cheetham and his wife, plus about twelve students of theology.

My lecture: on the religious situation in Germany. There is a

[176]

large audience—and tremendous applause. During the discussion period I receive a number of questions with detectable Nazi tendencies. At the same time there is a strong sense of "sympathy with the emigrant."

.

Claire and Guenther report most interestingly on Palestine. Everyone is fighting everyone else there. The capitalistic Jews in Tel Aviv, the Jewish communes (kibbutzim) which are turning Palestine, with its subterranean waters, into a second California; the Mohammedan Arabs who attack all Christians; the Christian Arabs who are full of hatred against the Jews; the English who always prevaricate, but finally stepped in vigorously on the side of Jewish capitalism; the Jewish proletariat, extremely powerful and dangerous. Guenther is optimistic for the Jews because the English need Jewish capitalism. Claire sees no solution: she feels that the Arabs are being treated unfairly. While in Palestine, Claire and Guenther were in constant danger of their lives. Once, the only thing that saved them was their Arab guide saying they were German Nazis. Hitler is a big man with the Arabs. Mussolini gives them money to spite the British. The Communists are severely persecuted. It is a witches' cauldron in which everything is reflected. Only Englishmen are permitted to bear arms. The Jews have founded a self-protective organization which keeps a cache of arms for emergency purposes. All the men in the settlements must do guard duty at night.

Dinner with red Capri. Long conversations, later alone with Claire, about various tensions. Claire rejects the dogmatic ties with Communism, feels unable to decide; nothing really appeals to her at the moment. Guenther's position is generally critical; he gives an excellent objective analysis. He thinks the German economy is changing from private capitalism to state capitalism. Private capital, he says, is being eliminated through forced government loans. There is no more credit. An economic catastrophe is not to be expected, though; at best the standard of living might go down. As for international politics, he believes that Europe will fall prey to Hitler without a fight.

Germany, 1971

HANNAH ALONE

A taxi driver who had survived imprisonment in Russia said, "I lost everything, but now it is good again." The war is discussed as one might talk about some ugly mischance. Everyone speaks impersonally, denying responsibility. The "Amis" are no longer mentioned, nor are the Nazis. Only occasionally do I hear a personal "We did a good job." As a rule, people use the pronouns "one" or "they." "They did it. They fixed it up and now it is good."

I was most surprised to discover that the post-war reconstruction of Germany often meant a literal rebuilding of destroyed or damaged structures. Churches were restored and city walls repaired exactly as they had been before the war. Even the moats around some of the old fortresses had been re-dug. For the Germans, physical restoration meant the restitution of a sense of national worth. But the newly restored city towers and monuments are simply a nuisance for modern traffic. Outside of the town walls, modern housing projects have sprung up. The days of the Third Reich seem to have disappeared from the people's memory.

In some weird way, Hitler actually did manage to win the race war. All the unpleasant, menial labor is performed by an army of workers imported from other countries. The Germans themselves have once again become a pampered people. Eating takes up a large portion of their lives. I ate in restaurants with endless menus filled with dishes from all countries as well as the traditional German specialties. And the Mercedes Benz taxis! Their distrust of an American citizen traveling in their country and speaking English with a German accent shows through only rarely: "An American guest, but her English is nix."

Rothenburg

At luncheon, I shared a table with a German couple and their surprisingly articulate twelve-year-old son. The father gushed, "We have it good." They had a house with a garden and swimming pool and had just returned from a two-week vacation. Another woman opposite me looked like a medieval portrait with her two or more white-skinned chins. It scared me to see these German types whose portraits I had so often observed in museums coming toward me out of the past. A likeness of Dürer's portrait of Pringsheim sat eating in a niche by the window. Next to him sat a blond madonna from the Rhine. A little farther away was a dark-haired Swabian beauty. And then there were the heavy, middle-aged mothers with enormous breasts, sturdy legs, and fine, blond hair with permanents, all wearing brightly colored print dresses. Beside each of them sat a father, the beer-bellied breadwinner and unquestioned master of his family.

A handsome fifteen-year-old guided a group of us through the medieval torture chamber in the town hall. He hadn't a shadow of a suspicion that the torture chambers of the twentieth century might have been far more terrible than the crude little room he was showing us.

I had rearranged my travel plans in order to be in Nuremberg for the Dürer exhibition. The first morning I had to stand in line for one hour just to get to the ticket counter and another half hour to get upstairs to the most important part of the exhibition. I was timid, not daring to get too close for fear of offending some other onlooker. The second day I forgot my fears and just looked at the paintings.

Dürer grew out of the Gothic age and into the Renaissance. Traveling widely, he became a patrician and citizen of the world. He had neither the religious fervor of a Grünewald nor the social consciousness of a Goya, but his craftsmanship was extraordinary. Dürer wrote a book about proportion which examined, in numerous drawings, the possibilities of the human face and its expressions. He drew a net of squares superimposed on a face to register different expressions as deviations from a norm.

There was a mercilessly realistic drawing of his old mother and a small one of himself as "The Ill Dürer" pointing to the place on his nude body where his spleen was hurting him. Among his many self-portraits is one *en face* (until then reserved for pictures of Christ), showing him with exaggeratedly regular features, long, curly hair and eyes glimmering green like a cat's. He was cool and self-possessed. I stood in awe of his technical skill, his ability to render perfect by the minutest details. Tolstoy employed the same technique in his work, describing the exterior world down to the last fringe in a dress, portraying the interior world by giving us the outside detail. Dürer was the master of precise observation but nevertheless impregnated whatever he painted with his own vision of the truth. I did not discover one shred of humor in his work.

West Berlin

Berlin is a city that had the guts to leave one of its principal churches—the Emperor Wilhelm Memorial Church—almost completely unrestored (though, to my chagrin, they did repair the clock). Next to the damaged church stands a recently constructed, octagonal meditation hall with blue stained-glass walls and a flat ceiling. It looks like a hat box or a candy box without ribbons. Fortunately, it isn't a bit as one would imagine Pandora's Box to have looked. But the madonna-blue meditation room is filled with an awareness of past atrocities. It has become a favorite with the hippies, who use it as a meeting place.

Berlin has several state museums, built by notable architects. And when I was there, a stunning new cultural complex, not unlike New York's Lincoln Center, was just being completed. I saw a performance of *Peer Gynt* there; I followed the play with excitement through to the last scene on the circular stage—the lowest point in the theater—which was ringed by spectators in consecutive raised tiers. It became the arena for a spectacle of human foibles: greedy rascals plotting on chairs in a desert, mocking dances and phantoms streaming out of cavernous Hell. Political ad libs delighted the audience.

I had a moving experience in the museums of Berlin when I saw the old masterpieces I had studied as an adolescent back in place and intact. Art had survived the holocaust. I felt whole again in Berlin, the city where I had spent my youth as an art student.

Spain, 1971

HANNAH ALONE

Seville

I walked to the cathedral, a huge Gothic church with high naves. The choir was filling with priests beautifully intoning the Litany. But coming out after the service with their lacy aprons tied around fat stomachs, they became Sancho Panzas with cunning, full-cheeked peasant faces.

I lingered in one of the church patios in a small orange grove lined with trees bearing golden fruit and fragrant blossoms. As I was about to reenter the church, I was held back by the sound of martial music in the street. I went in once more but the blaring trumpets pulled me outside again. A group of children and grown-ups had assembled and were waiting expectantly. Marching toward the church in the summer heat, four abreast, with heavily synchronized steps, drums and trumpets sounding, was a long column of smartly dressed soldiers in woolen uniforms and white gloves. They were carrying rifles. In front of the procession marched three soldiers: one held the flag; the two others, their drawn sabers. The noise was deafening; the power they exuded, the authority of discipline, tremendous. They marched into my orange grove, stopped and stood at ease, rifle butt by foot. A trumpet blast called them to attention. They re-shouldered their rifles while the color-bearer and his two companions goose-stepped into the church. They marched stiffly into a chapel to an open silver casket which lay before a golden altar for the Madonna of the Kings. Somebody beside me said, "They're paying their respects to their patron saint." A priest blessed the flag but the crowd was so unruly he had to scream for attention. The "Three Musketeers" rejoined their fellows, goose-stepping out of the church.

I overheard an elegant gentleman remark to his companion, "Franco may have eased up a bit, but once in a while he has to show he is still the boss, with the military at his beck and call." The only political comment I would hear in "mute Spain."

Later, I saw the soldiers being loaded into trucks. Now that they were no longer marching, they looked like a group of overgrown children, friendly but completely without authority.

On the other side of the river, atop a high cliff, I discovered the images of Sancho Panza and Don Quixote woven in metal, standing black against the sky. I sat down for a drink just as Paulus and I had done in Cairo. We had watched the mighty waters of the Nile from the same sort of tree-bordered cliff restaurant as this one overlooking Seville's gentler flowing river.

Granada

I rush to the Alhambra. Much smooth restoration. What most appealed to me was the only non-Moorish monument: twelve medieval lion cubs in the center of a fragile courtyard spouting water from their noses.

The Alhambra demands a knowledge of history. It stands unreadable between gardens and a ruined cloister. Its art is something the Buddha might have cherished, the art of dissolving the world into ornament. Flowers become ribbons, scripture becomes decoration. I was so relieved by the twelve lion cubs because they were not crocheted into the lacy pattern of the ornamental façades. I imagined for a moment I could dissolve the ornament if I could only find the first thread and begin unraveling each mesh of decoration until the plaster Alhambra would stand naked in empty embarrassment.

The Moslems, caught in the mesh of chance through their belief in fate, must have seemed just as inscrutable to the crusading Christian knights who had only their own faith in "making the world safe for Christianity."

Cordoba

An afternoon trip to the archeological museum, a building filled with fountains each whispering one thin ray of water.

The Christian gods are clothed. The mother of God resplendent in a blue and silver gown. Christ, carrying the cross, wears a black-and-gold-striped robe. The clothes of the Madonna are as sweet and pretty as an apple tree in bloom. Her face has become that of a doll. Glory without a personal image turns to trash, suffering becomes pornography.

The treasures brought home from the Americas by the Conquistadors were forged into snaky, twisting candelabra, golden ceilings, and pearl-embroidered vestments. The treasures went to make crowns for the queen to wear when being carried before the public, perhaps on a jewel-encrusted litter, which would make her bearers groan under the weight of its shining earthly wealth. The gold from one of the bookends against which the priests rest the gold-encrusted Incunabulum could buy a comfortable life for large numbers of Spain's ragged country people.

What interested me was the greed of the religious vision, the attempt to fill space with an infinity of imagery and leave nothing uncovered. The churches all seemed efforts to reconstruct Noah's ark: man and beast compressed into one structure overflowing with objects. In Cordoba's cathedral I found this same overcrowding in the choir carvings, restlessly filled in with intricate medallions portraying episodes from the Bible. There were two entire walls of these carvings enclosed by an arch overhead to prevent you from soaring out of the realm of objects into the sky of objectless meditation. And the columns in the Mosque serve to keep you moving horizontally through a forest of wondrous pink and blue marble trees. You wander from light to shadow and forget the sky. You are enmeshed.

A group of Spaniards stood obstructing the entrance to the Museum del Toro, leering at photographs of nude women. Here was unspoiled pornography. The husbands dared only fleeting glances while their wives stared defiantly and openly at the pictures. One was of a woman holding four oranges under her naked breasts. Another nude, her lovely back to the camera, stood surrounded by four raven-women dressed in black. Still another seductive young woman displayed swelling breasts and hips beneath a flimsy covering, while her face insisted on her innocence and sweetness in a complete separation of consciousness.

Madrid (The Prado)

In all the Goya paintings the eyes are prominent; soft, lecherous, unavoidable. I saw his self-portrait and felt possessed by those brown pupils, a male Mona Lisa, sucking in life, a man who paints whatever he sees within himself. His mouth was broad and fleshy, his ears were not small. But most striking of all were those eyes, eyes with one purpose only, to allow the artist to paint what they saw, even though it meant empathically experiencing the hellish sufferings of his subjects. I considered "Saturn Devouring His Children" on the boderline of madness until I saw the same theme done by an earlier master. Goya's "Two Old People Eating Soup" is a grim revenge on old age. How he must have hated old age and ugliness, how he must have loved riches and sensuous beauty, the softness of women and silk.

I dared to go and see Maja. Clothed, she is simply vulgar. But Maja, the nude, is the most beautiful body of a woman ever painted. The loveliness of her skin against the green cushions, the perfection of her breasts, the line of her torso down to her ravishing feet. Only the face is somehow doll-like and lacking in animation in both paintings.

Trying to revover from Maja's tenseness—she always seems ready to leap into a fierce dance—I walked to Titian's *Venus and Danaë*. His plump, heavy-hipped women, so sensuously wrapped in veils and softness, could never be imagined standing unsupported on such tiny feet.

I went again to the Prado and visited Maja once more and also "The Milkmaid," a strange portrait alleged to have been

Goya's last painting. The profile of the milkmaid is delicate, the face like an apparition seen emerging from a vapor of veils, a materialization as if during a seance. I found it deeply moving: a picture of health returning to an old sick master who has turned away from the mysteries of subterranean Hell-imagery into the clear light of a milkmaid.

A Bullfight in Madrid

After six bulls, enlightenment struck. I saw the earth as if from another planet, turning in the majesty of empty space, and on it the bull and his adversary, the toreador. Nothing but these two. The arena was the slowly turning globe, the bull and bullfighter gigantic sculptures viewed from all sides.

I had to squeeze my eyes together a few times before I could return to the spectator-filled arena. At this point, the question concerning me was "What does the bull see?" He reacts differently to different people, always turning abruptly toward his enemy, the one destined to kill him. The bull smells the horse as something animal-like, familiar. The banderilleros, with their swift dance movements and sharp darts, must seem like hornets swarming over him. The red paint around the inner ring would mean nothing to him, nor would the red of the cape. But its rapid swirling motions must fascinate and enrage him. Drawn into a mass of whitish soap bubbles, of black veils, of gray cotton masses, moving before him, he must ache to throw his thrust into it, to embrace it, to destroy it, to sink into it. At times, he seems to move with the rhythm of the cape. The toreador teases him then, guiding the hypnotized beast around him, making him thrust and miss, leaving him standing in abject dumbness before the cape. The bullfighter would even turn contemptuously away from his victim, who could only stand petrified, unable to use his deadly power against the toreador's exposed back. At one point, motion ceases and the two stand locked in silence, staring at each other before the last embrace. Dying, the bull emits a tortured cry and the audience sighs with him. Or he falls, dumb and heavy, with blinded eyes, trembling with one last convulsive shudder. The music takes up three mournful notes, singing the death of the bull, becoming gay when the triumphant toreador carries his prize around the arena; an ear or two, or perhaps even the tail. The crowd roars. It is *their* triumph, or *their* defeat if bull and toreador fail to perform.

Escorial and the Valley of the Fallen

After visiting the palace and equally hideous monastery, we proceeded by bus to the Valley of the Fallen, Franco's memorial and burial place for the dead of the Spanish Civil War. We sighted a cross, five hundred feet high, atop a craggy mountain. Pulling into a gigantic parking space at the foot of the mountain, we came upon an oversized semicircle of columns. When a lady and I set out to find the promised restaurant, we discovered there was none. We settled down on a chair beside a Coca-Cola machine to watch the driver play at dice. Stone figures at the foot of the cross were larger than life size. An elevator went up through the rock to the cross. I did not go.

I was disappointed in El Greco, and his many copies of his own work. They became mushier and more elongated, the beards of the apostles fluffier, the faces so full of cheap ecstasy. For me, Velasquez was the realistic observer; Goya, the satirical romantic. Velasquez seemed to express the Spanish landscape on a cool, clear day. Murillo seems to have painted through misty raindrops flowing down a window pane. Goya met the whole human scale.

One afternoon, tired of appraising the work of the great, I walked through two mediocre museums searching for a smile. I found none. Eyes cut out onto a silver platter, a meal before death, an announcement of treason, Mary with the corpse of her son. Even the Madonna and Child theme was burdened by the foreshadowing of coming affliction. Christ on the cross was only the occasion for a pornography of suffering. In one abominably realistic sculpture, painted red blood poured out of Christ's nose. Strange heads of Christ painted *en face* with green shadows, a deathly pallor, and no smile. There were saints with their heads chopped off and all sorts of wheel-twisting horrors.

It must be an extraordinary sight for an Eastern man to see these tortured creatures, the representatives of our God. The Buddha may expose himself to all sorts of trials, but his image remains untouched. Never are his features disturbed by extremes of emotion. Neither cloying melancholy nor physical anguish ever disturb the serene lines of his face. If I had not learned to hate this expression of Christianity before, the Spanish baroque would surely have taught me.

Santander

Blown-up baroque space disappeared when I entered Santillana. The Monastery Museum with its Romanesque cloister and early capitals brought tears of happiness to my eyes. Looking at the sculpture, seeing the proportions of faces and bodies, made me suddenly aware, in an illegitimate rush of emotion, that I was a part of this circle of culture and race. It was a feeling that I would never before have admitted.

The caves of Altamira were a disappointment until our party came to the Cave of the Bison. I do not speak or understand a word of Spanish, but through the inflections in the guide's voice I understood and was elated. I threw myself down on a burlap-covered clay bench and stared up at the low ceiling where deer and bison grazed. They were proof that our ancestors were not quite so primitive as we wish to make them out.

Barcelona

The city looked crooked from my seventh-floor hotel room overlooking the port. I had been in Barcelona before with Paulus on an Italian liner which had stopped there for a few hours, allowing us to go ashore. I remembered a long walk along the harbor to our ship, but I could not find the transatlantic dock. There were sailboats, small ships, and a commercial dock with cranes. I never recognized my harbor.

I took a long guided tour of the cathedral which I remembered vividly from my trip with Paulus. Two chandeliers like white crystal flowers against a golden ceiling. A fresco of Ferdinand and Isabella receiving Christopher Columbus—"the first tourist," remarked the guide—after his initial trip to the New World. The "Indians" and the foreign beasts he must have described or brought home were also shown. I understood the Old World glory growing out of Columbus's voyage from the wealth they eventually brought Spain.

I saw, for the third time, the Gaudí Templo de la Sagrada Familia, which I had visited with Paulus, and still did not take to it. It seems such a sordid creation, squashed out of a mushy tube. I felt no better about it even after separating out the parts added after Gaudí's death. I did get to the park with the Gaudí waterfall, but my neighbor on the tour bus and I enjoyed Tibidabo. We got to talking about Gurdieff, Ouspensky, Yoga and such and walked together in the amusement park peering at photographs of Montserrat, Seville, and a bullfight. Afterward, we went to the Picasso Museum. The city seemed inexhaustible. It is a city to live in and to explore. The Barcelona of my trip with Paulus and this new Barcelona became one city. Suddenly I found myself very happy.

Columbia University, 1968

THE OWL OF ATHENA

She had felt estranged the first time she walked alone around the campus, dressed as she was, grandmother-style, in a white coat and hat. Young women in miniskirts, hair flying.... Young men with long hair—often tied in a pony tail to keep it from blowing in the wind—and beards, invariably ragged and dirty. Looking unwashed seemed the style. Outside the still unfinished campus gates, the police were setting up barricades. An enthusiastic old officer with an intelligent face was directing a group of sullen young policemen unloading the barricades. Even they, however, were absorbed in the job.

"What are you hoping to accomplish," she asked one of the cops—"driving them out of the occupied buildings?"

"I hope so," he answered with a sigh. It was difficult to tell what was meant by the sigh, whether it was a negation or an affirmation of the job he had to do.

A small group of blacks had assembled in front of the gates at the Broadway entrance. They were huddled around a tall young man who was speaking to them in an authoritative manner. Two were fingering their identification cards uncertainly. The authoritative one said, "They won't let us in the Amsterdam gate so let's try here." He remained in the background while one of the group presented his I.D. card. But a plainclothesman at the gate turned him away.

The old lady moved nearer to the tall black. "Only Columbia people can get in," she said, taunting him. He remained silent. "You should know that only people who belong to Columbia University are allowed inside," she repeated stubbornly.

This time he answered, but in an offhand way, just to humor the old lady in the forbidding bourgeois attire. "And just how was I supposed to know that?"

"Why are you here then?" He took a step toward her and she retired behind a police officer who turned to look at her questioningly. "It's a group from another campus; they weren't allowed in," she said. The Negro looked at her with open hatred now and she returned his stare, her eyes full of challenge. They locked eyes for a short eternity. Finally, he laughed, in exasperation, and turned away. She smiled.

"Rap Brown got in and so did Carmichael," remarked a man beside her.

"What do you think about it?" asked the old woman.

"I'm just an observer, I'm impartial," was the reply.

She walked on. The police were still unloading barricades. "Catch," called a cop to his colleague, making as if to throw one of the heavy wooden planks . He sounded healthy and strong.

"Take care," she said, smiling. He waved at her with his wooden plank. Around the corner, half hidden in a little niche, stood a young policeman. The old woman approached him. "What are you people doing here?"

"What we are doing is nothing." He sounded bitter. "Absolutely nothing. But even so we'll be blamed. And likewise if we do finally do something." A man joined them. The three smiled at each other. "At Normandy," said the policeman, "we had reason to fight. But what in hell are we doing here?"

"One hundred and sixty-seven cops," said the civilian wonderingly, "are distributed all over the campus, from Amsterdam to Broadway and on the side streets, and still nothing happens." He shook hands with the policeman and so did the old lady.

"Thanks for the smile," she said vaguely, and wandered on.

She joined the crowd back at the gates. Somebody asked, "Why should they be thrown out?"

She answered, "Because there are thousands of other students who want to get in." The "somebody" shrugged his shoulders and evaporated into the crowd. She tried asking somebody else the "somebody's" question. He was a tired-looking man with an intelligent face wearing a white hand-kerchief tied around his arm, either designating some office in this emergency or perhaps meant simply as a sign of peace. Before he could reply, a wedge of militant blacks, dressed smartly in berets and black leather jackets, approached them. Marching in a loose column, they were pushing straight through the crowd, making the "thought people," who were standing around con-versing, move to the side. But the old lady refused to budge. Instead, she walked straight toward them, saying "Excuse me" in a polite voice, but forcing them to divide for her. At that moment she did not feel at all like one of those "intellectuals." They had been so busy analyzing the situation that they hadn't even noticed when the blacks pushed them off the sidewalks.

The cool rationality of Athena was sorely missing on both sides. No owls of Athena on anyone's shoulders. Black crows perhaps, diving to find seeds in the rubble while the world was burning. She again passed the tired man with the white armband and turned around to make a new appraisal. It seemed to her she saw, resting precariously on the shoulder of this intellectual, with his bloodshot eyes and shabby dress, the faint shadow of a small, gray-and-white-flecked bird. The militants would have no owls on their shoulders but would march hawklike and proud behind their authoritarian leaders who would demand only to be obeyed. But this one, this shabby man with the ghost of Athena's owl on his shoulder, would not obey orders. . . .

The old woman walked through the campus gates. Some members of the faculty had formed a kind of neutral blockade around the seized buildings. They were preventing the police from entering and at the same time forbidding students from either entering or leaving. The professors stood silently or in quiet conversation. They would not raise their voices even during a heated confrontation when they were called upon to protect a small group of blacks who had booted their white radical friends out of one of the buildings, making them, so to speak, "second-class revolutionaries." "Out of the way, 'cause here we come," been the cry of the black students. Accompanied by television cameras and radio announcers, they had marched in and chased the other students out. And how shabby the white students had looked! They did not mind being shoved aside. "Excuse me," they said, hands in their pockets, looking surprised. "Hey, I'm with *you*, man. I don't want to fight."

She remembered a story a friend had told her about a subway rider who had been attacked by three youths. One of the kids had crushed a cigarette out on the man's shoulder. "What happened then?" the old woman had asked.

"Nothing," her friend replied, "he didn't take offense and it just went by as an inconvenience, an everyday inconvenience."

So they were shoved aside. Some of the students became a little impatient and one of them booed when the blacks made a statement from a second-story window. Baskets of food were hoisted up to them while the faculty stood by impassively. The funny thing about this campus was that you could not really assemble a crowd. The people remained individuals, refusing identification with the group. They could not fight for themselves, whereas the blacks could and did. The militants had a goal, their movement was young. The whites became unified when marching in the South with Martin Luther King, for example. But was there cause here to march? Though they were largely sympathetic with the blacks' cause, some students were beginning to feel the militants might be going about things in the wrong way.

A group had collected around two police officers. Jokingly, one of the cops began stamping his feet saying, "Get mad, you guys, get mad." He was poking fun at the football players, all muscles and power, telling them to keep cool and not use their strength in senseless aggression. The old woman passed by smiling.

"What are you laughing about?" asked a bystander.

"There's an owl on his shoulder."

"On whose? What owl?" He looked at her as if she were nuts and, at the same time, began gazing nervously about, as though there might be an owl after all.

"On the policeman's shoulder," she said, laughing, "the owl of Athena, the bird of wisdom." She passed a group of students listening to an older man. "Who is he?" she asked the person next to her.

"A very good teacher, one of our best physicists."

She overheard only a fragment. "The problem is extremely complex . . ."

"Good," thought the old woman, "that, at least, is a start." Aloud, she said to no one in particular, "But it is not enough to go into a monastery and think."

A shabby-looking man with an owlish face responded. "But this is a monastery."

"Yes, and there are two kinds of people here. Those who think and those who act. The active ones have the power now, but can they still be reached by the power of thought?"

"Perhaps we have bungled badly," said the owlish one, "maybe we were fools not to act forcefully. But perhaps we have also been wise fools."

The old woman gave him a look of pure surrender and cried out, "I do love you, you wise fools, you foolish wise men. You will be the ones to perish or be swept aside, but how I do love you anyway."

She walked up the library steps. A manchild was standing there, clean, thin, with pensive eyes and a well-trimmed beard. In his hand was a bunch of yellow flowers. He handed her one and she took it. That seemed a good enough language for both of them. No words were necessary.

San Francisco and Berkeley, 1972

Graffiti (on the walls of a free clinic)
1)
You cannot always get what you want
but you sometimes get what you need
2)
Lost in a maze I find my way
by following the dotted line
and come to a land
where insanity is a standard of living
3)
I find it facilitates
the usage of every day mindfucking
to read every line backwards
4)
Wanted; Jesus
by the F.B.I. (for long hair)
5)
Insofar as you have suffered
"Black" is a matter of historical experience

Seminar with a black professor
"Love" is using someone
"Hate" being unable to use
Manipulate what you hate

[197]

Alienation as a human calamity
If your experience is destroyed
your behavior will be destructive

Indictment (stenciled on a sweatshirt)
I am frustrated
I am alienated
I cannot communicate

On guilt feelings
The pupil confesses to his master. He was
masturbating with a bottle in his rectum.
The master: "What kind of a bottle?"

On social action and personal growth
Buy a new suit of clothes and act
as you have never acted before

Go through the motion of action
until you get to the essence

This has been today's news. If you don't like it, go out and make
some of your own.

On learning
You become by learning, not by diving into the abyss of your
own feelings.
In the Orient, the master imparts wisdom.
In the Occident the teacher is an expert at communicating facts.

On truth
Truth belongs to the individual.
Truth is changeable, honesty is not.
You must find your own truth with the help of wisdom and fact.

ON ZEN AND NON-ZEN

The Japanese Zen Master taught about the selfless self, about enlightened Buddha nature. "Intuition," he said, "is the memory of Buddha nature." He spoke of the "changeability of every human concept." People have memory, but time, like the river, is only succession.

The attentive students became children, listening with fairy-tale eyes. Their predicament was to be trapped in "imaginary time." Now they were experiencing thingless emptiness.

The hippies had wrestled with the thing-orientation of their civilization. Now, before them, pointed out by the Master, lay the *tabula rasa,* outside time and emptied of illusion. But to follow they must leave their worldly possessions behind along with their fathers and mothers. For the Buddha demands "non-thingness." Destruction of values will become the creed of his American followers. They will go forth to live in the desert in one of those vast stretches of no-man's-land. And even if the land turns out to belong to some capitalist, this fact is apt to be ignored, for capitalism belongs to thingness and, of course, one wishes to overstep all such illusory divisions as property boundaries. They will find their clothes and cooking pots in the garbage dumps of civilization and will probably hang these second-hand pots and pans on the walls of the cave in the same way it was done in their mother's kitchen.

The students have a greed for the void. It is, however, not non-illusion they seek, but extinction. What these disciples of "non-Zen" cannot comprehend is that Zen does not destroy, it leaves the things of this world unmolested. War is in one's mind, peace is nothing to affirm or negate. There is no ego. One does not see the moon, one "becomes one" with it. All substance is the same, all substance is one. Only the human's shape distinguishes him from the moon. The moon is merely our human concept and human concepts are illusory. This kind of disillusionment is a dangerous toy in the hands of children. For our civilization is not made for oneness but for the particular; the chain reaction of betterment. The spiral is our constellation. But the silent center around which the hurricane rages is not our abode. These students, in their Western activism, cannot realize how much time the Master spent whirling in the fury of the storm before he could enter the silent eye. They believe they can purchase satori with a few lotus-posture sittings and meditations on thing-destruction.

Out of the mist of thinglessness looms the figure of Charles Manson who walked down one of the branch paths of meditation which leads to the liberation of id impulses, to action, to power drive and the desire for extinction. The path he chose leads into the disposal-hole of the cosmos, where the dead matter of stars falls into black nothingness without hope of reentering the creative cycle of the universe. Strangely, scientists seem to have discovered this cosmic garbage heap in the so-called "black hole" where burnt-out matter collapses into something so dense it defies light. In the "black hole," the individual, distinctive quality of matter has been lost.

Scientists were still in the process of confirming their observations when Manson was practicing the black magic of creating an empty oneness out of "human matter," destroying the borderlines between individuals, merging separateness into a black oneness. There was no enlightenment in enlightenment anymore, no nirvana, just dead matter.

Manson managed to dissolve the separate personalities of his followers into a kind of collective personality that negated the very concept of individuality. He also succeeded in breaking down the barriers between night and daytime feelings, that is to say, between the physical and psychological merging of man and woman that occurs at night and their return the next morning to separate daytime existences.

Manson was able to arouse and nourish a continuous desire for subservience in his child wives. His women's ego feelings collapsed into inarticulate heaps of submission. The Nazis were similarly successful in destroying the sense of self of many of the inmates in their concentration camps. But where the Nazis used sheer brute force, Manson employed a kind of sexual hypnosis to enslave his followers. At some point in his development, Manson

[200]

must have come to identify sex with death. Sex became for him a method of extinguishing the cosmic configuration called man.

What failed those girls were the words "*I am*"; their consciousness of themselves as discrete individuals. Manson had wrapped them in the vapors of "Maya," the great indistinction, the leveler of the sense of I-ness. He pushed them into a "black hole" where they became indistinguishable from each other and from any other organism, and not only during their moments of sexual intercourse with him.

If they had tried, perhaps the girls might have found individuation in Christ. Or Buddha might have helped, if they had turned to his image and pronounced the sheltering pledge, "I take my refuge in Buddha." Even a middle-class American faith in rationality and common sense would have saved them. It was presumably the creed they had been brought up in. Perhaps it seemed shallow to them and incapable of reaching emotional depths. But it is nonetheless clear that a woman needs the white light of reason and self-determination to help her survive the horrors and ecstasies of dependency that is an integral part of her role during sexual intercourse.

THE TIBETAN LAMA

I went to a session with a Tibetan lama. There were about twenty disciples sitting in the lotus posture pronouncing *OM*, some religious gymnastics, and an unsatisfactory speech by the lama on Tibetan teachings, which was hampered by his appalling lack of English. The lama was immersed in the problems of temple buying. It seemed he was in the process of buying a house that was to be transformed into a cloister with no money but the pledges of his disciples. The pledges seemed very high to me, considering that his followers were students, who had left the university for his sake, with no other resources than their intermittent checks from home. They looked dirty and haggard and were crowded into a house that was run as a commune. The students were forbidden to smoke, eat meat, or use drugs or alcohol. It seemed rather peculiar to me that these students, who had rebelled against the system and given up all the comforts of civilization, were now kneeling at the feet of a teacher who had all the cunning of a peasant when it came to the art of persuading his pupils to make material sacrifices. Spiritual awakening seems somehow irrelevant when the search for peace becomes an awkward struggle to pay fees to a greedy monk at the expense of one's intellectual training. The students have forfeited their birthright—that all men are created free and equal—and have downgraded themselves to the status of labor ants, employed to build a hierarchy they can hope to enter only as eternal servants.

THE NURSERY

I visited the nursery for retarded children located in a wide street on the outskirts of San Francisco. The concrete driveway in front of the garage was used as a play area for the children. There was also a small, enclosed yard with a sandbox, swings, and a slide.

The large rooms of the old house contained little in the way of furniture. In one room, a sofa, some small cardboard tables, and mini-chairs had been set up for the kids. In another, a sandbox had been placed on a heavy wooden table. In still another room, abandoned dolls lay on the floor beside a pile of children's books and building blocks.

The nursery's director was a friend of mine. She and I stood outside on the concrete driveway watching a little four- or five-year-old black boy who was walking about with a shambling gait. He was emitting all manner of incoherent noises which, I guessed, were unsuccessful attempts at pronouncing one-syllable words: "No!" or "Don't!" or "Give me!" My friend offered him a tricycle but made no effort to show him how to ride it. The little boy only tried to roll it down a slope and through a break in the low stone wall which surrounded the nursery.

My friend kept repeating, "No, no, no," monosyllabic as the

boy's own gibberish, while pushing the tricycle back every time he approached the slope with it. She made no effort either to help or redirect the little boy. I went over and helped him mount the bike. The supervisor disapproved, and we talked about it at length. She felt no helping hand should be offered, no attempts made, for example, to get the boy to speak. My friend was waiting for him to develop the first signs of speech on his own. She thought it wrong to interpret the boy's gibberish as the first slurring attempts at speech.

Inside, I sat down in one of the children's chairs and watched the little black boy rampage around the room overturning empty chairs. Some building blocks were lying on one of the cardboard tables. I got up and placed one block on top of another. The boy immediately grabbed one of the blocks, threw it to the floor, and then pounced on another chair. He watched me out of the corner of his eye as I sat down on the sofa. Suddenly he jumped up onto my lap and embraced me. It was difficult to tell whether he was being violent or affectionate. I hugged him back until somebody took him from me.

In the next room a tiny girl was throwing a temper tantrum. Another little girl, who had obviously been dressed with a great deal of loving care, picked up a burnt-out match and held it directly in front of her eyes between two tightly pressed hands. When a nurse took the matchstick away, the little girl simply found another one and repeated the procedure. This time, the nurse, irritated, left her alone.

I accompanied one of the mothers (the mothers of children at the nursery serve as helpers under the supervision of a registered nurse) outside to search for a missing boy. "His only wish is to escape," she said sorrowfully. We found him crawling around at the far end of the property looking for a hole in the garden walls. After being carried back into the house, he continued to search for an exit, creeping along the wall from room to room.

A little girl lay on a sofa, her tiny face pale as death, her features delicate as those of a wax figure. Her coloring reminded me of the waxen pallor of a schizophrenic I had seen in a hospital with my psychoanalyst nephew.

The mothers had come to pick up their children. I followed

[203]

the tricycle boy with my eyes. He was held firmly by the hand of a fat, ugly, disheveled black woman. The moment they had crossed to the other side of the street from the nursery, she dropped his hand and began to run away from him with surprising swiftness. The boy ran screaming after her.

When I returned two years later, I discovered that the girl who had held the matchsticks so close to her eyes now wore glasses. The tricycle boy had been permanently institutionalized.

THE POET AND THE RINGMAKER

In the restaurant, the poet began ordering wine without asking leave of his hostess. He reminded his wife of a wine they had enjoyed on another occasion. She remarked sullenly that this time *she* wanted to taste the wine, too. I tried to explain the function of this little ceremony—nothing more than an attempt by the host to ensure that his guests receive only the best. She brought up Women's Lib and the argument ended with two wine-tasting guests.

The woman was red-cheeked and well scrubbed. Her husband looked ash-gray, with wisps of hair on his face and head. He spoke quickly and with a curious accent. He was Polish by birth and had lived in Scotland for quite a while. Presently, he and his wife were sharing a three-room apartment, in a low-income San Francisco housing project, for which they paid only sixty-five dollars a month—half the normal rent—with the government taking care of the rest. They received food stamps and, in fact, took every possible advantage of the government, naturally denouncing it all the while.

I visited the couple at their apartment to select some rings (the wife made jewelry), and admired the well-furnished, uncluttered rooms. The husband showed me one of the poems in a collection of his work entitled *The Poet's Book*. The words were printed entirely in capitals, making the poem seem somehow like a woodcut. It described his wife's passion for scavenging through the garbage, searching for discarded treasures of the rich. She still

[204]

spoke with great seriousness of her days as a trash buzzard. To me, the very idea of collecting things from a garbage heap seemed repulsive. The idea of bringing into my house the incompletely extinguished emanations of an object's previous owner revolted me. But, one day, said the wife, she had found herself unable to move from room to room, so cluttered had the apartment become. She decided then and there to throw out almost everything, keeping only the "essentials." She stated that her greed for possessions had simply died and her husband confirmed this. Even he now gave away his most valued possessions—his books—once a year.

I selected two flat stones, one brown and one gray, for the two rings she was to make for me. Both rings had special significance for me. One showed an ascending moon guiding a cat safely through a thick forest; the other, the sun, symbol of liberating joy. The former was an Ojibwa Indian good-luck charm, the latter a Parsee sun-worshiper symbol of happiness. Tremendous work and research were invested in these simple rings. They were lovely and I treasured them for a long time.

The poet had read Jung and viewed things from an unworldly but well-informed perspective. He mentioned the poems of certain prisoners, poems which seemed to him of great importance. What struck me as strange was the crowd with which these young ones chose to people their world. The poet and his wife were anti-social, but cared for the lives of prisoners. That they themselves might fall victim to the misery of prison life was unimportant. They played Buddha, who had tried to help thieves and robbers. But, according to Buddha, the thief and the murderer would eventually find their own inner freedom. The thief would tire of thievery, the murderer would give up killing to take the path of spiritual salvation. But these young people were concerned only with the social aspect of the problem. They were concerned with the moral reasons for the prisoners' confinement.

New Haven, 1975

THE MONGOLOID AND THE HEALER

Our mother Ishtar, half hidden behind a veil of aquatic plants, stood upright at the bottom of a stagnant pool, surrounded by swimming tadpoles sucking at her breasts.

"Look at the tit-suckers," said my friend, staring through the glass of the aquarium, "aren't they just like Don's mongoloid friends, always greedy for the touch, always hoping to come alive through contact with another's skin. Tit-suckers . . ." he repeated.

I had just spent two hours in a school for sufferers from Down's syndrome. My friend Don was head teacher there. What caused me to make the most impossible travel arrangements to visit the school? I think now it must have been the memory of the San Francisco nursery where I had been dissatisfied and frightened by the teachers' "no touch" policy of refusing to guide the children and leaving them entirely on their own resources. Here, the opposite approach was taken. The program was based on scientific research, but at the same time took into account the need for a direct empathetic line of communication between teacher and pupil. It had achieved results heretofore believed impossible.

I was shown into a medium-size classroom divided into three sections, with each section corresponding to a different level of achievement. Near the doorway, a dedicated-looking gray-haired woman was speaking with infinite patience to three males of indeterminate age. Except for their faces, which looked much

[207]

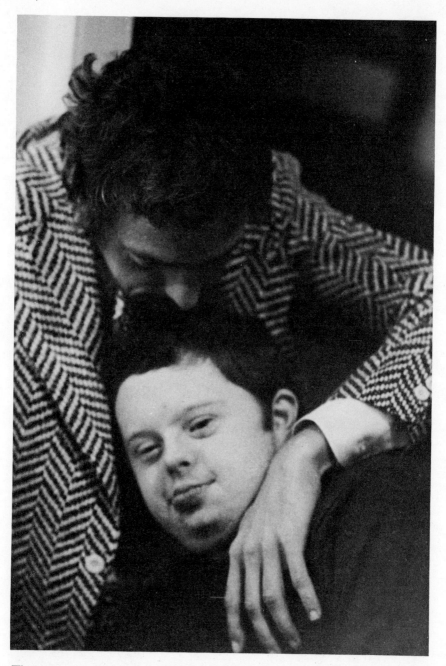

The mongoloid and the healer (*M. Kilbourn*)

older, they might have been taken for twelve- to fourteen-year-old children. One of them turned to look at me and I was shocked by the age in his face.

As my friend had said, you could explain something to them for a hundred years without making the slightest impression. One of these unteachables came forward with one of his drawings. It was a crickle crackle across the page, colors in dark-red, brown, and black. The hand holding the crayon had moved mechanically across the paper. There was no beginning, no end, and no attempt at design.

The gray-haired woman was trying to explain the distinction between a penny—a unit that represents one unit of value—and a nickel—a unit that represents five units of value. I believe there was some reward for those able to answer her questions on this subject, but her pupils' responses, even when correct, seemed to have been made at random.

At a table, in another corner of the room, six pupils of uncertain age had assembled. I observed my friend Don moving from student to student, touching, talking, laying his arm around one boy's shoulder and, for an instant, guiding another's hand. All six were very much aware of him and of the quietness and attention his presence demanded.

Don proudly showed me the correctly filled-in social security card of one of his pupils. At the moment, he explained, he was preparing a test. Each student had to write five words that begin with "b" and one word that starts with a capital "B." They succeeded with the small "b's" but finding the word beginning with a capital "B" was too specific a task for their abilities. One of the boys, during a short period of attentiveness when he was not leering and grimacing, said, in a tone of deep satisfaction, "I get a good education." Under Don's protective arm, his grinning and babbling were transformed into quiet attention. The teacher had rested a gentle finger on his pupil's arm. It was a healing gesture. For the short space of a breath sucked in and held, the boy had become whole.

Don sat down beside a blind boy who suddenly became the happiest child on earth now that his teacher was with him. The pupils' expressions would change rapidly from comparative

[209]

liveliness in Don's presence to senseless grins in his absence. When they were alone their faces would assume the blank stare of absolute noncommunication.

When traveling in foreign countries, in the street or in any place that drew my attention, I used to stop and stare. Later, when my friends would ask me what I did on those long and lonely trips, I would reply that I was opening myself unreservedly to a place's foreignness, letting my conscious and unconscious minds drink in my surroundings; using my "cat-intelligence," meeting my insights directly, without the interference of language. It was so much easier to express oneself with a smile, a frown, or a nod; jumping from *Sonnengeflecht* to *Sonnengeflecht*, vibrating directly through the channels of feeling and circumventing the intellect. But the mongoloids' eyes, blank as an impenetrable wall, took in nothing and would remember nothing.

It was painful, after leaving the world of the retarded, to discover a similar incompleteness of face and gestures in so-called normal people in the street. I saw the twin of a retarded boy who had brought me his copy of a painting on the Adam and Eve theme. For the boy, even daring to draw had been a liberation, but his picture already showed all the signs of a mechanical repetition. How often would the boy and his double in the street repeat themselves without feeling? Or the empty leer of another mongoloid man-child—when might it become the grimace of unbridled aggression?

I knew what Don meant to his "children," but what did they mean to him? If Don felt it possible to become whole through a relationship with another being, then why would he choose to relate to these deprived "children" who could never blossom into full humanness?

Only the asceticism in Don's face prevented him from being the incarnation of a classical sculptor's vision of beauty. His hands and feet seemed to be carved from ivory and his touch was pure compassion. Swift and decisive, he did not seem in the least bothered by the presence of so many confused mental vibrations.

It had been a tremendous effort for me to understand the

[210]

inarticulate and disorderly mind of the mongoloid. I tried to comprehend wordlessly, through intuition, in the same way I dealt with my cat, blinking directly from human eye to cat eye, bypassing the intellect. But perhaps there was too much of their enigmatic darkness—their incompleteness—in me to allow understanding. Perhaps it was impossible to understand them empathetically. Maybe only someone who had freed himself from any identification with their weaknesses could be of help to the mongoloids. Or perhaps Don was only reliving a childhood dream. Wishing to be rescued by a friendly hand from the stagnant pit of his childhood, hoping to be guided to a life of new possibilities, Don may have identified with his own saviour. Even so his relationship with the mongoloids was mutually rewarding. Their feelings of bliss at being liberated from the prison of noncommunication were joined by his enchantment at pouring his own life force into other beings and seeing the gates spring open to a lost and unknown wholeness.

.

I had met André before my first visit to the school when I stepped outside to see my friend's garden, the care of which, according to Don, was his own personal therapy. It was a warm May afternoon and the trees, flowers, and blooming bushes reminded me of Lochner's medieval painting of a garden in Paradise. The Holy Mother and the Christ Child resting in a low-walled garden, each blooming plant painted with loving distinctiveness. . . .

Sitting in a straight-backed chair in the sun was a squat figure wearing a blue shirt. He was moving his arms and hands, reaching into the air or occasionally taking a sip from the glass perched on a table in front of him. His hand movements seemed synchronized with someone else's. I saw Don sitting some distance away in a low folding chair under a shady tree. It was toward him that André's fluttering gestures had been directed.

André was red-haired with a somewhat misshapen, pear-shaped head. He sat earnestly and with dignity in the midst of Don's lush garden. I came over eagerly, Don joined us, and we had an unhurried conversation. André could not speak articulately but I thought I could distinguish garbled sentences and ideas in his gruntings. The three of us went inside for dinner. André performed beautifully. His manners were perfect and he followed our conversation attentively with what seemed to be some understanding. Before the meal he had helped set the table and when he came to get me to come to dinner he was careful to let me go first through the door. In general, he was a quite dignified if occasionally giggly companion. I asked to see some of his paintings and he promptly got up and showed me every single one, proudly but without a trace of vanity. After seeing the drawings of his classmates I began to understand that André was in every sense a professional. His sense of color and design was infallible and there was no sign of his physical incompleteness in any of his work. There was only a feeling of balance and wholeness.

The next morning at the school he was awaiting me eagerly. I had been warned in advance not to confuse him with another mongoloid boy. For André had an imitator who resembled him physically. This boy, not understanding the form he was imitating, produced only feeble, insensitive copies of André's work.

André was to draw me. I sat down on his right and emptied myself spiritually, disconnecting my brain waves from his, that I might follow his inner process without interference. To do otherwise would have been like entangling oneself in a net of live wires. He assumed an expression of intense concentration as he reached for one of his pencils. He drew my face, figure, and hair—this last a little thicker than it really was—without hesitation or correction. I thought he might even capture my "aura." Glancing up occasionally, André drew my eyes and my mouth—without showing the teeth—and carefully followed the pattern of my dress. I felt entirely connected to his artistic effort, feeling I was helping him to perform as he did. By the time he gave me to understand the picture was completed we were both exhausted. But Don came over and told him to finish it up using an assortment of yellow pencils. André began, a bit listlessly, to fill in the drawing with several shades of yellow, selecting with dream-like certainty what seemed to him *"la couleur juste."*

[212]

Perhaps his attention span had become exhausted. In any case, Don sent him away on some trivial errand and I left soon afterward. But before leaving, I touched André once while standing behind him, very lightly on the arm, just as I had seen Don touch his pupils. Unexpectedly, he reacted to my touch as though it had been a mild electric shock.

New Harmony, 1975

I passed the sign at the park entrance:

THIS PARK WAS CREATED FOR PAUL JOHANNES
TILLICH DEDICATED BY HIM PENTECOST 1963 AND
COMMEMORATED TO HIM PENTECOST 1966 UNDER
THE DIRECTION OF THE ROBERT LEE BLAFFER
TRUST WITH ASSISTANCE FROM ROBERT ZION AND
HAROLD BREEN–SITE PLANNERS JAMES ROSATI–
SCULPTOR–THE GEOLOGY DEPARTMENTS OF RICE
UNIVERSITY AND INDIANA UNIVERSITY–STONE
CONSULTANTS AND RALPH BEYER–LETTERER.

Another placard read: "New Harmony designated a registered historic national landmark, 1965."

When I returned to New Harmony in the spring of 1975 the trees in Tillich Park, now more than ten years old, stood twice a man's height. Near a man-made lake, the Rosati bust of Paul Tillich stood free against the meadow under a serene morning sky.

The paths in the park had become narrow ribbons. I turned to Paulus's gravestone and its inscription:

And he shall be like a tree planted by the rivers of water that bringeth forth his fruit in his season. His leaf also shall not wither; and whatsoever he doeth shall prosper.

Farther on, atop a small mound encircled by Norwegian firs, the family, Jane Owen, and a few close friends had placed Paul

[215]

Tillich's ashes in the ground, unenclosed in any separating urn. I saw myself, a ghost in a blinding mirror, throw a small jar of his ashes, not bigger than my ring finger, into the ocean at the American Indian burial ground in Esalen. I remembered how he had loved the ocean as I stood under the high cliff and watched it restlessly hollowing out the rock. And, one day in India, in the early morning light, as the sun rose through the haze, a yellow rayless ball, I surrendered another portion of his ashes to the Ganges. The last "memory" of Paul Tillich's physical being I delivered into the hands of the Dalai Lama. Now, it seemed to me, his spirit was our noble inheritance.

I followed the circular path through the firs, reading the inscriptions on the high and low granite slabs. Jane Owen had taken selected passages from his work and had them carved into the hard rock of the slabs in large letters. The trees would grow, the stones would become part of a natural design and, in time, it would be as if the inscriptions had been carved by the wind and rain. I liked best the passage on miracles:

Today we know what the New Testament always knew, that miracles are signs pointing to the presence of a divine power in nature and history and that they are in no way a negation of natural laws.

Jane Owen has told me that when she first saw me she "caught the laughter" in my eyes, and everything had seemed all right after that. Paul Tillich and I had just arrived from Evansville to dedicate Tillich Park. It was Pentecost and we felt quite at home in the little house which reminded me of an old Hessian farmhouse. It stood on a village street, surrounded by lush meadows and rolling hills. Nearby, at the village outskirts, a river flowed beneath the overhanging branches of tall trees.

Jane Owen had shown us the old houses she had restored, keeping the original furniture and preserving window and wall space, but adding the modern comforts of electricity and indoor plumbing. I remember the majestic poster bed in our room, which was so big I had to use steps to climb in and out of it.

[216]

Windows with tiny panes looked out over an unpaved, tree-shaded street.

Jane Owen wrote:

> Individuals, civic groups and the state of Indiana are now working together to preserve the heritage and to assume deeper value for the next generation.

But she had begun the project alone and proceeded single-handed for many years.

When Paul Tillich came to dedicate it, the park was little more than a rain-soaked parcel located between the Red Geranium Inn and the slope toward the farmland. At the narrow end of the planned park stood the heavy gilded portal of Philip Johnson's Roofless Church. It baroque doors were by Lipschitz. The Johnson-designed red-brick wall was unadorned but for a balcony providing a view of the surrounding countryside. Space could flow from the main street through a simple gate and expand infinitely upward into the Roofless Church, uncramped by window, wall, or enclosing roof. Under the mushroom of the tabernacle a sweet Virgin Mary arose from a heart-shaped shell, formed not unlike the chestnut I had found under a tree, split open to reveal a glistening, golden-brown fruit. I felt the same affection for Lipschitz's Mary as I had for "the little sweet brown one," as the people of Montserrat had named an ancient brown Madonna in one of their churches in which the legend of the Holy Grail had not yet expired.

On that first trip to New Harmony and on every succeeding one I paid at least one visit to the Rappite cemetery. When they sold New Harmony to the Owenites the Rappites stipulated that their church was to be dismantled and the bricks used in constructing a wall around the unmarked graves of their brethren.

The walls of the Rappite cemetery and of the Roofless Church brought back the memory of the ageless stone wall at the rock garden in Kyoto, with its carefully designed pattern of stones on sand, raked into rippling waves. Paul Tillich and the

Paulus and Henry Luce, with Claire in the background (*J. Loengard*)

Paulus speaking at New Harmony in 1963

Philip Johnson's Roofless Church (*James K. Mellow*)

Paulus with Jane Owen

The burial stone at Paul Tillich Memorial Park in New Harmony

The bronze sculpture by James Rosati of Paulus, New Harmony

Zen Master Hisamatsu had spent a timeless hour there reflecting on participation and identification; comparing Eastern and Western modes of thought. In my memory the three walls and Paul Tillich's New Harmony burial site had been woven into one spiritual event; a meditative pause to be approached with devotion.

When I telegraphed Jane Owen to request that Paul Tillich's ashes be allowed to rest in the park he had dedicated at her invitation, among the trees the three of us had selected together, the response was a generous yes. At the time, I had no idea of the difficulties involved in arranging such a project. I am very grateful for Jane Owen's splendid handling of all difficulties and I feel Tillich Park was the right place for him to come home to.

Jane Owen had had several ideas for Tillich Park, but when she visited us in East Hampton on the two and a half acres we had transformed from a potato field, complete with chicken coop and a small yard, to a "park" filled with an exuberance of stately trees, we found ourselves talking about trees as a memorial for Paul Tillich. Jane generously promised to plant every tree we had mentioned in that wonderfully jubilant conversation: the chestnut tree, the birch, the beach, and the fir.

Jane Owen had James Rosati in mind for a bust of Paul Tillich and Rosati did, in fact, agree to do it. So for one precious sitting, Paul Tillich met the artist at his studio in New York. I was worried about his health at the time and the doctor had warned him against the visit to New York. And, had it not been for the assistance of an anonymous friendly New Yorker who left his shoeshine concession for a moment to help carry the suitcase of a struggling old man from Pennsylvania Station through a tunnel to the hotel, Paulus, with his weak heart, might have been in bad trouble.

Time was getting short. I wouldn't be able to walk through the labyrinth to the little temple at its center. I turned and entered the bookstore, trying with the help of a friend to thread my way through the manifold events which had shaped New Harmony.

Hanging from the ceiling of the rectangular room were pictures the size of a Chinese scroll with inscriptions showing the

[222]

history of New Harmony from the time of the Rappites through the Owenites right up to the present and Jane Owen's resurrection of the past. History stared me in the face in the form of cultural achievements, some memorable and others long forgotten. The Minerva Society, America's first women's group, had been founded in New Harmony. New Harmony had put into effect the first laws regulating child labor. And the Owenites had organized one of the first major geological surveys of the Western United States. It had extended from Indiana to Oregon, and rock samples were sent back to be analyzed at the Owen laboratory in New Harmony. The town had also been an important cultural center with its own opera house, which Jane has now revived.

It was a delight to see all the books. Every conceivable subject from the past through the present was covered in the displays. There were ancient cookbooks, books on animal husbandry, on landscaping, soil conservation, arts and crafts, architecture, music, and flowers. New Harmony, when I visited it, seemed virtually drowned in flowers.

I walked to the banks of the Wabash to say farewell to the river which felt so near the landscape of my home country. The trees would continue to grow and the water, constantly renewed, would keep flowing lazily along the river bank under this dreamy overhang of spring-born leaves. The Spirit would find new words to express the needs of the day; new words to guide us through the mazes everywhere. . . .

All was well in this time and this place as I boarded the flight that would bring me home.